THE SECRETS OF AGELESS AGEING

THE SECRETS OF AGELESS AGEING

DR KAREN WARD

BEEHIVE

Published 2022 by
Beehive Books
7–8 Lower Abbey Street
Dublin 1
Ireland
info@beehivebooks.ie
www.beehivebooks.ie

Beehive Books is an imprint of Veritas Publications.

ISBN 978 1 80097 029 8

A catalogue record for this book is available from the British Library.

'Now and Then' by Sophie Hannah reprinted by kind permission of Carcanet Press, Manchester, UK.

Designed by Jeannie Swan, Beehive Books
Printed in the Republic of Ireland by SPRINT-print Ltd, Dublin

Beehive Books is a member of Publishing Ireland.

Beehive books are printed on paper made from the wood pulp of managed forests. For every tree felled, at least one tree is planted, thereby renewing natural resources.

For the very special young people in my family –

Jack and Emily Di Pizzo, Charlotte, Robyn and

Nico Ward Pratt – may I be the type of elder who lives my life

as an inspiration to you all and encourage you to be the best

you can be for the future of our small,

beautiful country and our world.

CONTENTS

ACKNOWLEDGEMENTS

A huge thank you to:

My love – John Cantwell, my husband, my friend, my colleague, *fear críonna, saoi.*

My elders – Dell, my mother, Anne, my godmother, and Agnes, my mother-in-law – wise women all.

My earth family – the extended Ward, Whitty and Cantwell clans. I thank you all from my heart of hearts for your support and love.

My spirit family – Bryan Ward, my father, and all my ancestors who have lived, loved and gone before me, having shaped the world I live in today.

Team Beehive Books – especially the visionary Síne Quinn, eagle-eyed editors Mags Gargan and Leeann Gallagher, patient design whizz Jeannie Swan and PR supremo Pamela McLoughlin. I so appreciate your faith in me and this book, especially with its eleven-year gestation!

Huge thanks to all my wisdom-gathering helpers, especially Mandy Fitzgerald and Máire Moriarty.

Míle buíochas, a thousand thanks to all the Moon Mná – your sisterhood is invaluable and a constant source of inspiration to me. Also to all the powerful and immense Slí an Chroí community.

Finally, and most importantly, to the muses of this book who inspired me to write in many weird and wonderful places including Cusco, Peru, on a plane over and back to

Australia, in a tent in West Cork and at our kitchen table in Smithfield, Dublin in 2011. Inexplicably they then ground the whole glorious process to a halt for eleven years, before once more nudging me forward as an older and wiser woman to complete in 2022.

INTRODUCTION

IT ALL STARTS IN OUR FORTIES

I used to think that old age was something I would experience in my seventies, but in my mid-forties I discovered that the ageing process had already begun. To my surprise, it was rapidly encroaching on many aspects of my life. Rather than feel trepidation, I decided to find out more about the inevitability of ageing and try to do something about it, if possible. There had to be some way to ease into my older years with the grace and vibrancy I had seen some women and men possess. What secrets did they know that were not common knowledge? Through my research, I realised that the kind of older woman that I would become depended on the foundations that I put into place while I was still young enough to do something about it.

In ancient times older people were often called the 'elders' or the 'wise ones', or some such respectful name. This term encouraged younger people to revere these members of the community, and to treat them with honour and dignity. In some indigenous cultures the tribe does not actually take you seriously until you are in your sixties. However, in our modern society it seems we are the exact opposite – we worship youth in all its glory. While media and advertising might be partly to blame for this, we also have to admit that our collective consciousness focuses more on the first phase of our lives. Now that people are living longer, our society needs to become more aware of the benefits of ageing.

During my research, I often asked adults if they would like the body they had when they were a teenager. Most reply, 'Of course.' I then asked if they would like the mind they had as a teenager. They quickly replied, 'Definitely not!' There is a fabulous saying that 'youth is wasted on the young'. Did we ever truly appreciate our bodies, our masses of energy and our enthusiasm for life in our youth?

There are plenty of life events to look forward to in the first half of our lives. After forty what is left? For many, it's a sixtieth birthday, retirement, illness and death. I think you'll agree that that doesn't sound very appealing. However, we do have the opportunity to change the way we view the next third of our lives – a chance to fulfil our wish list and experience everything we've always yearned to do. We can choose to be positive and proactive, creating new milestones that excite and thrill us before we get to the stage that they are only dreams and not the reality we can make them. The choice is ours and ours alone.

WHY READ THIS BOOK NOW?
Full of tips on how to prepare wisely, this book highlights the various aspects of our lives that will change over the coming years. It emphasises the need to embrace the exciting, sassy elder you dream into being of your own volition. These changes start much earlier than we think, whether we are ready or not, so the time to begin is now. I am honoured to help you along the way with a plethora of advice from my years as a counselling psychotherapist working with holistic energy therapies, as well as some sage words from very wise women and men who have made the journey already and paved the way for the rest of us.

The idea for this book came while walking in Dublin's Phoenix Park – one of my favourite ways to unwind. Since we have only a small yard at home, I refer to this local stunning place of beauty affectionately as 'my back garden'. To be quite honest, I was fairly intrigued when the inspiration for this book came to me so strongly. Indeed, in an hour the whole concept was mapped out before me. I laughed and asked myself: who would take me seriously as a forty-something (at the time) talking about old age and how to prepare for it? But the idea wouldn't go away. I acknowledged that it had come from a deep soulful place within and, therefore, deserved my attention. Coincidentally my holistic health and counselling psychotherapy clients then began to mirror my idea with similar thoughts in our therapeutic sessions. However, it was my body that showed me in no uncertain terms that I was definitely onto something. I noticed a change in my energy levels, a thickening around my waist and a drooping of my eyelids.

When I spoke to friends and family of different age ranges about my idea, they identified with the notion of positive and mindful ageing. When I thought about the title *The Secrets of Ageless Ageing*, I began to consider the concept as one of 'divine guidance', which I feel when I open up my heart and Celtic soul, living in the moment. As an ageing adult, I wanted to find a way to tap into the positive elements of both youth and experience and combine the two. I thought about the wonder and playfulness of childhood; the gorgeous confidence and invincibility of my youth balanced with the maturity of my life experience so far. I felt that I could encourage readers to also combine these elements of their life in order to benefit their future. Having fleshed out the bones of the book, I then stopped. Somehow, I felt that I didn't yet have all the life experience I needed, nor the gravitas to publish until I was over fifty. In the intervening time, I was awarded my doctorate of philosophy, went through the menopause and became more comfortable in my own skin. I reached that crucial stage of life when I began to care less about what people thought of me. When I started my sixtieth year, I knew the time had come and I am delighted to say that the contributors who I had invited to share their fascinating reflections on ageing agelessly updated their wise words eleven years later. Their heartfelt answers are interspersed throughout this book.

WHO ARE WE?

Our midlife is often the time when we come to face who we really are, which can be a daunting prospect. This is when people take stock of what happened in the past and start to think about what they hope for in the future. It is usually at this midway point that existential questions emerge, such as 'What's it all about?' and 'Who am I?' Some people prefer to avoid this period of their life by keeping eternally busy, living through their children or hiding behind unhealthy comforts. Some feel stuck in a rut with their current job, but are afraid to change or consider alternatives, worrying about their prospects elsewhere. Others might lament their youth, focusing on any regrets they have, including wasted opportunities.

In some cases, the old adage that 'life begins at forty' spurs people on to new goals. Many take valuable time to reflect on what their dreams are as they enter this stage of life. Some go back to college or change careers or begin new hobbies they had always dreamed of pursing. Others take the opportunity to focus on their health and start to exercise more. Many people run their first marathon in their forties. Statistics also reveal that more people in Ireland and the UK are becoming parents in their forties than ever before. All these changes are positive ways of entering a new decade and taking stock of the future.

How often do we look up to the shakers and movers in society, thinking that someday we'll be the top dog, doing interesting things, living life to the full? At some stage we realise that all the old cliques – 'This is it', 'It's now or never', 'You only live once' – are true and were coined by people who felt this important tipping point. Personally, I believe that it is never too late to pursue your dreams – though why wait? We can either listen to these gentle nudges and mature into wiser and insightful versions of ourselves or ignore them and run the risk of feeling stuck or empty.

WISDOM FROM THOSE WHO KNOW

I thought that to make this a really interesting read I would invite older and wiser people to offer their sage advice. I asked them to share what they wished they had known earlier in life, to talk about their regrets, and to pass on wise tips they would want to give to their children, grandchildren and future generations. To put all this valuable wisdom into context, I asked for a few vital pieces of information: their name; where they lived and now reside; their age, of course; and what they would term their occupation. Then I asked them two questions:

1. What do you wish you had done or started earlier in your life?
2. What are you delighted you did or started earlier in your life?

Initially, I intended to interview people in their seventies, eighties and nineties, but then I realised that if I began to feel a shift in my physical, mental and emotional state when I was forty-six, it was important to also include people in their forties, fifties and sixties. I decided to talk to a broad range of people from very different walks of life – including some well-known names – by email, letter and in person. It was an intriguing exercise, and I learnt plenty of valuable information that really gave perspective on what life is all about. I was totally mesmerised by the reaction and the myriad of answers. I had either met, knew of or was inspired in one way or another by most of these amazing people. Throughout the book, I have inserted their tips and thought-provoking answers, gleaned through years of trial and error, on how to grow older while becoming wiser and happier.

I didn't steer any of the interviewees towards a particular subject; in fact, for those I personally interviewed, the answers came spontaneously from the heart. I have written them down verbatim, so you can 'hear' their words directly. I had already mapped out the thirteen chapter titles and, so,

I matched each person's offering to a specific chapter. There were funny, poignant and interesting contributions that gave me food for thought. I trust that you will think so too.

Throughout the book, I have highlighted tips to try – practical advice for you, the reader, to consider as a way to prepare for or enhance the experience of growing older. You'll see these clearly as you read through each chapter.

Sometimes I'll illustrate a point by giving an example of client scenarios within my clinic work. I wish to point out that I have changed key details to preserve confidentiality and indeed most are an amalgamation of a variety of client stories.

Chapter One   MIDLIFE OPPORTUNITY

MIDDLE AGE

It's a fascinating label, isn't it? 'Middle age' brings connotations of people who are 'past it', settled into a boring routine having lost the zing of life. A few years ago, I was shocked to realise that double forty-two equals eighty-four, a very respectable age to, as Shakespeare said, 'shuffle off this mortal coil'. When I was middle-aged, I thought that I'd better start fulfilling my wish list soon, as I wouldn't be around forever. Although that all sounds slightly morbid, it was actually more of a wake-up call than rejecting a label I felt foisted on me by society.

Around this time, a number of very interesting clients arrived at my clinic presenting with no specific problem, just a general sense of flatness. Coming to psychotherapy or counselling is not something you do on the spur of the moment. It takes both financial and personal commitment. It also takes bravery and soul-searching. My clients, a mix of men and women, were all successful people in employment with a comfortable home life. During our sessions together, we holistically looked at all aspects of their lives. Every one of them honestly examined their relationships, work situation and family situation. Of course, there was some work to be done, but overall things were running relatively smoothly. Yet something was missing. Then it began to dawn on me: all the clients ranged in age from thirty-nine to fifty years of age. They viewed their lives as exciting and developmental up to this point, but now felt that they were facing a long vista of repetition followed by old age and death. If this sounds dramatic, then read on.

MILESTONES
If you think about it, from our childhood to our fortieth birthday there are amazing markers in our lives. Most of us have schooling followed by training for a first job, a career, first love, relationships, eighteenth, twenty-first and thirtieth birthdays, perhaps marriage or partnership, perhaps children, and many holidays. There are a lot of life events to look forward to in the first half of our lives; however, after forty or thereabouts, it may feel like there is nothing appealing or inspiring left. But there is so much more if we look at those around us who are only coming into their stride, with wisdom and life experience enhancing all they do.

We are lucky that for the first time ever the majority of us, in the western world, are living longer than our ancestors. Historically the average age of death for a working man in Europe was approximately sixty-seven years. In 1889 Germany became the first nation in the world to adopt an old-age social insurance programme. German Chancellor Otto von Bismarck set the age of retirement at seventy, though it was changed after he died to sixty-five and that was copied by the American social security plan. They figured that two years was enough time for working men to put their affairs in order; however, the world we live in now is very different and, consequentially, many are living into their eighties and nineties. The standard retirement age in Ireland and the UK is now sixty-six and in the United States it is sixty-seven. For some people the thought of retirement means boredom and brings fear of illness and death. For others, however, it brings opportunity – time to travel (often using their free travel pass), catch up with old friends and embark on forgotten hobbies.

My male clients were faced with younger hotshots at work winning the accolades and chasing the promotions. For one of them there were no promotions left, as he had gone as far as he could go within the company. Some of my female clients were seeing their children pursuing their dreams and feeling the effects of not having had the time to look after themselves physically. Is it any wonder that I only had three clients in this position brave enough to realise that there must be more to life than that bleak 'is this it?' feeling and to seek to find another way?

TIPS TO TRY
Check in with yourself and see how you view this middle stage of life. If you have sailed through it with aplomb – well done. Now is your time to share how you did that with others. If you are yet to face this pivotal time and are unsure, then ask those who are older and seem to be thoroughly enjoying life – what do they know that you need to glean now? If you are having feelings of depression or anxiety about it, take a conscious step back and make a plan. Remember there are more than enough of us who have made the transition favourably.

POSITIVE POTENTIAL
It dawned on me that perhaps 'middle age' is one of those terms, like 'spinster' or 'bachelor' that does not have a very nice ring to it. Perhaps we could start by collectively changing it both verbally and mentally to 'half way' or a 'midpoint' in our existence. We could regard it not as a negative but as a potential positive. At this stage most of us have had a lot of life experience and some people are fortunate to have a little deposable income. We could use this point in our lives to make lots of new life events to look forward to.

A good friend was recently bemoaning the fact that she hadn't been dancing in ages, and as a result felt decidedly old. Two people in our company responded in very different and fascinating ways. One replied, 'Oh, discos, yes, I really enjoyed that phase of my life.' The other told us about her Zumba keep-fit dance class at the local gym. It is important to know that we all have phases in our lives and that we need to let certain aspects go to allow new areas to open up.

There is no reason why we can't reconnect with old interests if we choose to later on in life. It is difficult or virtually impossible to have a vibrant clubbing life while rearing children or working hard to deadlines, but if you love dancing, why not incorporate it into your exercise regime? Many men, and increasingly women, love the excitement and camaraderie of five-a-side soccer, while not having to find the time to get fit enough to run around a full-size pitch.

We all have the opportunity to change the way we view the second half of our lives. It can be an exciting chance to do the things we've always wanted to do. By using our creativity and a bit of imagination, we should be able to make a start and see how far it takes us.

WORDS OF WISDOM
Name: Jo McCulloch.
Country of origin: Scotland.
Country of habitation: Dublin, Ireland.
Age: Eighty.
Occupation: Lorry driving, working on the trawlers, the merchant navy, the army, a circus act. I am retired now.
1. What do you wish you had done or started earlier in your life?
I wish I had done a parachute jump for the thrill of it. Do it now while you are young!
2. What are you delighted you did or started earlier in your life?
Getting married twice to two lovely people. My first wife, Jeannie, died after nineteen years together. I'm married to Carmel for twenty-six wonderful years now. Also, I learnt to read and write myself as an adult. I'm thrilled to bits as life is so much richer now and more fulfilled.

FULFILLING A DREAM

I once watched a UK reality television programme where people could win £500,000 to fulfil their dream. All they had to do was explain what it was and why they wanted to pursue it. Thousands of competitors applied, but only four finalists were selected for the last round. One was a woman who worked in a supermarket on the checkout and dreamed of being a sommelier. In all her years of having this dream, she never once asked to be moved from the main checkout to the wine department cash desk. She never did any wine courses, even though they are relatively easy to find in any town or city. The second and third finalists were a couple, who fancied opening a restaurant in Greece, just like the film *Shirley Valentine*. Amazingly, they had only been to Greece once. It hadn't dawned on them that if they holidayed there every year since they thought of the idea, they would have learned the rudiments of the language and made local connections. The final man wanted to be a guide in a safari park in Africa. He was a window cleaner, who spent most of his spare time at London Zoo and various UK safari parks. The animals practically knew him by name! He pored over library books, reading and learning all about the care and maintenance of his favourite species. He had also saved up and gone to Africa three times. He only needed the prize money to pay for the expensive procedure of getting a visa and a licence. Guess who won? Of course, he isn't cleaning windows anymore or if he is they are in his new African home. I was mesmerised by the show. I couldn't believe that the others hadn't even tried to follow their dreams.

A lot of people are so hung up on the daunting process of ageing that they feel they are too old to pursue their dreams or they are so fixated on the fact that there is some type of obstacle in their way that they don't see the most obvious pursuit or path is right there in front of them. Sometimes all it takes is for a helpful friend or colleague to state the obvious.

MOTHER EARTH

Not so long ago in villages and towns that were smaller and less populated, we would have grown all our food and exercised daily walking to and fro to gather local produce and well water. The rhythms of our life would have been close to and inextricably linked with nature.

In our modern world, we can spend hours or even days without going outside to feel the wind in our hair and the earth under our feet. So many people come to the clinic for stress management and really the very best teacher is a few steps away. Mother Earth is the expert in helping us let go of any worries or cares. Have you ever gone for a walk to return refreshed, renewed and totally recharged? Walking outdoors is a fantastic exercise because it is natural, free and you can do it anywhere.

I often walk up one side of the River Liffey and back down the other into Dublin city. A friend commented that I'm not really in nature there, but in the smoggy built-up concrete jungle of a city. I challenged her to come with me and observe. We saw six swans, a heron, three ducks, large fish and a robin in the space of a twenty-minute walk in Dublin city. Not to mention the joggers, walkers and people we saw en route. She was amazed. At one point we saw what looked like two young lovers holding hands and running laughing together. We both smiled; however, as they got closer we saw that they were at least in their fifties. We really laughed. How brilliant – playtime and exercise with huge dollops of mature love thrown in. Inspirational!

Remember no matter where you are, the earth is always below you and the sky is always above you. Forest bathing is now a recognised phenomenon and many therapists give their clients an option to schedule their session indoors or outdoors.

TIPS TO TRY

Perhaps this is the time to take stock and reconnect with the best stress-management counsellor of them all – Mother Earth. What about growing a few herbs in pots, sowing your favourite flowers in the garden or even considering an allotment to harvest vegetables for your family and friends? Then, on the subject of food, you could take it a step further and start the soothing task of bread making. I also know a few people who get great satisfaction once a year cutting the fallen branches from their garden to make firewood for the winter. The solace we derive from nature is immeasurable – from fresh air for health, heartfelt moments with stunning landscapes and soul-stirring birdsong. Whatever you decide to do to connect even more with nature, be sure to listen deep within and then make it your own.

WORDS OF WISDOM
Name: Philippa Haine.
Country of origin: Originally British. I lived many years in Ireland.
Country of habitation: I now live in Sydney, Australia.
Age: Seventy-nine.
Occupation: I was working as a radiation therapist in Dublin. I'm now retired.
1. What do you wish you had done or started earlier in your life?
I wish I had stayed longer in school and studied harder. I would love to have been a vet. I always loved animals.
2. What are you delighted you did or started earlier in your life?
I'm so glad that I had my children in my twenties when I was young and enthusiastic and could cope! Now, of course, I can really enjoy my grandchildren. Also, I am grateful to my parents; my mother for introducing me to classical music and my father for encouraging the wish for a lifetime of learning on all subjects.

Chapter Two   PHYSICALITY

THE SIGNS OF AGEING
The joy of maturing, knowing who we are and where we fit in life with a sense of being comfortable in our own skin means we have grown into ourselves in the best possible way. Reaching a point where we appreciate the wisdom of our life experience while still retaining the glorious wonder of a child is a beautiful balance point to aim for. Naturally, though, there are inevitable signs of that maturity especially as our physique changes to match our sagacity.

I used to think that the signs of ageing were crow's feet, laughter lines and weight changes, and I was right. To my amazement, however, I never knew or thought about drooping eyelids, 'bat wing' arms or wrinkled decollétage. Now I know why neck jewellery is so popular for women of a certain age. I realise why fashion for women over forty flows from the bustline and why there is the trend for men to hang their shirts over their jeans.

Around this time, the proverbial penny dropped about fancy lingerie. As a young woman I didn't really understand what all the fuss was about and assumed there would be a time when I would explore this option. Little did I know that when I did, I would need it the most – to prop up breasts that were rapidly sliding south of their own accord and to hide increasing lumps and bumps. I am blessed enough to know that my husband loves me as I am and wise enough to know that I am still me, no matter what my body morphs into – but do I really want to see my own fat ridges in the middle of a passionate embrace? No, thanks. This is where the stylish underwear really holds its own, pardon the pun. I feel great as the satin and lace covers a multitude. Good for my figure and great for my self-esteem.

TIPS TO TRY
As a woman, when was the last time you had your bra size checked? As we age, our underwear should change to match our older shape. Around menopause, including perimenopause, our breast size usually increases, so this is a good time to have a professional assess what you need. Most department stores have a free service that is fast and friendly. This is not a daunting experience at all; in fact, it is a good habit to maintain and an experience in self-care. Fancy lingerie is for sale in low-cost shops too, so this doesn't have to be an expensive purchase.

As a man, have you adjusted your trouser size as you age? Try to avoid having the waistband over your abdomen, which can look juvenile, or under your abdomen, which means you'll constantly have to hitch it up. Most menswear shops will be only too happy to help measure you for the exact size that will be most flattering.

DRESSING FOR YOUR AGE
I didn't understand the full meaning of this until I attended a lecture given by a professional woman in her fifties. She was an excellent speaker and had great posture and a fabulous figure that she obviously looked after. I was amazed at my reaction to her look, which was echoed by both a man and a woman sitting behind me, who I couldn't help overhearing. She was dressed in the manner of a much younger woman in clothes that you might see on a twenty-five-year-old. She did have the figure to carry it off but somehow to me it didn't look

right. The weight and gravitas of her wise words were at odds with her look. I sat with this for a long time and wondered why it felt strange to me. Was I too focused on what I thought she should be wearing? Was I boxing her into a category that was my perception of how a woman in her fifties should look? Was I envious of her? I wasn't sure. Recently I went out to buy my summer wardrobe and purchased short dresses that any twenty–thirty-year-old could also wear; however, this year, something felt radically wrong. That look just didn't seem right and I wasn't 'in my skin' so to speak. I gave away my new purchases to a younger sister and went out to shop again for a different and more sophisticated look that I felt suited my age and enhanced my self-worth.

Sometimes I don't hide the changing parts of my body when I dress but show them off. I started to love and enjoy my body as it ages. I look in the full-length mirror every night as I undress for bed and appreciate my naked form, including all the wobbly bits. After all, they are part of who I am. I smile and ponder about the fact that I am more comfortable with my body now, as it is ageing, than when I was younger and slimmer. I have come to accept myself, the beauty that shines from the inside out.

If you assume that buying new clothes will cost a fortune, depending on your circumstances and budget, there are a number of large retailers who stock reasonably priced dressy, casual and active wear with accessories. Nowadays we are conscious of fast fashion and its effect on the environment and so turning to charity shops is a wise alternative. Full of sartorial treasures and interesting accessories, they help you to feel good when you spy a great bargain knowing your money has gone to a great cause. It is also a terrific opportunity to offer these shops a bag of clothes or accessories of your own that you haven't worn in a while or simply don't fit or suit you anymore.

TIPS TO TRY

Designers for the over fifties know how to style this age range. The next time you are treating yourself to a new item of clothing you might consider long sleeves to cover looser upper arms, mid-calf skirts to cover older knees. It is worth investing in slightly more expensive longer-lasting garments that are style classics and won't go out of fashion. With added fripperies that nod in the direction of that season's fashions, a whole look can be created easily. A dark tailored suit for men is very flattering especially around the stomach and abdomen. Be savvy with the style of clothes you seek; for example, go with colour to be eye-catching and looser cuts for ease of movement.

Another way to garner new clothes and enjoy a night or morning of fun is to arrange a clothes swap with friends and colleagues, perhaps from your book or bridge club or local community organisation. After all, one person's trash can be another's treasure.

WORDS OF WISDOM

Name: Brenda Ryan.
Country: Cork City, Ireland.
Age: Seventy-eight.
Occupation: Fabric shop sales assistant, now retired.

1. What do you wish you had done or started earlier in your life?

I love baking for pleasure but I never learnt much about the icing side of things. In the autumn or winter time I got great enjoyment from watching Delia Smith with her easy, down-to-earth, common touch, showing how she could decorate lovely cakes. I wish I could have done that when I was younger.

2. What are you delighted you did or started earlier in your life?

I worked in Hickeys fabric shop for many years and some of us as young women started to make rag dolls and dresses from the remnants that I would take down to the Mercy hospital for the sick children, especially the ones with leukaemia. We found out that some would lose their hair and their First Holy Communion veils would not fit. One friend made soft cotton bandanas that we decorated for them. I am so glad that I was part of that – I still continue to visit today. It helped me learn to be happy within myself. I often think of my mam Maisie's wise saying whenever I might have been downcast. She would say, 'That'll all pass and you'll be alright.' She was so right with her good advice for life.

INVISIBILITY

I have often heard people in their fifties and sixties say that they are invisible and I wondered what that was all about. Now I know. I get glimpses of it on days when I potter about in my dress-down clothes with little or no makeup on. This is usually when I want to go into town for specific shopping and am in a hurry. I don't want to meet anyone and be social. I just want to purchase my shopping and scoot home. Inadvertently I am making myself invisible and it works. There are distinct advantages to being invisible when you want to be, as every famous person knows, since it allows one to go out in public unnoticed. So that chap you thought looked a bit like your favourite screen star probably was him wearing a tightly pulled down beanie hat.

On those days I'd become aware of men and women surreptitiously glancing in the direction of other younger, pretty women and literally not seeing me. It felt like instinctively they knew I didn't rate, I wasn't a contender. This is much in the same way that flowers show their bloom to the bees when it is pollination time but the bees are not attracted to them when they are beyond their flowering reproductive mode. You could say this is a sad state of affairs and there should be a grieving process for the fact that we are past our prime. Then again it depends on what you mean by this term. It might have been starting a career, finding a life partner or having children previously when you were highly visible in the world. Now there are other aims in life, not as known or talked about but well worth pursuing.

TIPS TO TRY

Speaking of invisibility, how often did we bemoan our current weight only to discover years later, when perusing old photographs, that in fact we looked terrific at that time? Enjoy yourself as you are now. Your family and friends love you as you are. If you really want to lose those extra few pounds then do something about it. Don't complain to your loved ones. They are probably too polite to tell you to stop but I bet their eyes glaze over if they hear you talk about it a lot. Remember it's not all about being trim but more about losing weight to be healthy and to stay active. Drinking plenty of water, having breakfast and not eating after 7 p.m. will help a lot. For more details and an opportunity to follow a simple week-long holistic cleanse, see the appendix at the end of this book.

HAIR HEROES AND HEROINES

I'm watching vibrant older women and planning now how I want to look when my hair changes colour completely. My friend Eimear has the most gorgeous long platinum hair and another friend, Juliet, has a flowing mane of grey hair that is amazing. They are both for me goddess-like in their beauty. I'm growing my hair now so I'm ready to join them in my sixties too. The last time I consciously grew my hair was for my First Holy Communion ceremony when I was seven years of age. How coincidental that I am doing it again for another significant phase in my life.

I'm also carefully watching the colour of my hair. It was a coppery red colour as a young woman, and then it started to darken to a more brunette shade. I love the colour of brunettes, but on other people. I am not and didn't aspire to be one. I wanted to find a more natural alternative and so began my quest. I didn't have to search very hard to find a natural rinse that was a great interim for my look.

I've noticed that my hair colour is changing again; there are whitish hairs in there now. I'm lucky that the redheads in my family go a nice pepper-and-salt shade of light red, which is when I intend to stop using the rinses and go completely natural. I remember the mother of a friend having the most beautiful black hair when we were children. Then literally overnight she became a blonde. It was a total shock to everyone and it took a while to get used to her new look. Of course, the reason she had to do it was that for years she was a slave to her hair. She had to colour it every few weeks when the grey showed through. Finally, she didn't want the hassle anymore and realised that, as a blonde, the colour difference would be slight and she could wait much longer before colouring.

 TIPS TO TRY

In your local health food shop, you'll find a range of natural hair rinses that have no ammonia, parabens or resorcinol, and less peroxide. The range is for men and women, and suits anyone with a sensitive scalp. Perhaps, like me, you don't like the idea of strong chemicals near your head. These ranges have natural organic vegetable and plant extracts, and they also do permanent colours that cover grey hair and lighten hair up to two shades.

If you have dark hair, subtly change the colour little by little over the years so it is a smooth transition from dark brown to light brown and eventually blonde rather than a huge change. Unless, of course, you want to go for a dramatic effect. It must have been a huge relief when well-known older men started to shave their thinning locks and go sexily bald. Sean Connery and Yul Brynner paved the way and eliminated the comb-over forever!

No matter your age, a good haircut can do wonders for your appearance and confidence. It can also be inexpensive as there are lots of hairdressing schools with final-year students looking for models. They are closely supervised by their teachers, so you come out with the style that you requested and a cut for free. The same goes for colouring, highlights and balayage.

REJUVENATE YOUR LOOK

Have you ever seen someone whose makeup, hair or clothes are old fashioned? It is as though they are stuck in a time warp, having kept the same style since their youth. Make-up can date us hugely so it is worth visiting a beautician for advice every five to ten years, especially since our skin tone changes as we age. Most department stores have cosmetic counters where the staff are only too happy to demonstrate their wares and might offer to do a free makeover if they have time.

We need to look at the whole area of skincare too as the tone and elasticity of our facial cells will change as we age. It is wonderful to see so many men discovering the benefits of looking after their skin and hair too. If as a young man this wasn't the norm or considered fashionable, move with the times and change now to explore this wonderful self-care area.

TRANSITION TIME

I wondered about a milestone that would herald crossing the line between being middle-aged and becoming an older woman. For me, it was wearing reading glasses in public for the first time. I vividly remember discovering that I couldn't read the newspaper anymore without some serious squinting. For most people this is usually around the age of forty-five. I bought a cheap pair of magnifying glasses and only used them for reading newspapers and books; however, menus began to be a problem too, so I went for an eye test and the good news was my long-range vision is excellent *but* my short range had deteriorated, so I'm described as long-sighted. It really helped me to talk to others close in age to discover they were experiencing something similar. I keenly felt the sense that there was no turning back once I started to wear glasses in public. It was a visible sign of ageing that was irreversible. I knew, though, that eventually I would have to wear them socially. Finally, the great day arrived and we went to dinner with friends. When we reached the time to peruse the menus, with great fanfare I reached into my bag and pulled out my funky leopard-print reading glasses. Instead of this being a big deal, a hilarious farce ensued as the other couple asked could they use them as well since they were also having trouble reading the small print. We all shared my glasses, making me feel part of this new phase of life rather than different and alone.

 TIPS TO TRY

Try and wait as long as possible before having to get glasses by making sure to use good lighting for reading and exercising your eyes. A simple way to exercise your eyes is by visualising a large clock in front of you. While keeping your head straight, move your eyes only (not your neck or head) around the clock stopping at each five-minute point for a few seconds. Then do the same anticlockwise. It will feel a little strange at first as the muscles of your eyes have probably not been worked out for a while since we are so used to turning our heads rather than moving our eyes. When the time comes, don't be too proud to invest in a good pair of glasses that suit your face. You can always try out an inexpensive pair of magnifying glasses from a chemist shop first to see the strength that you need. Eye tests are not expensive and many opticians reduce the cost of them if you buy glasses there too. Eventually you may even consider laser eye surgery, which is becoming more affordable now.

RESEARCH ON AGEING

Dean Ornish, the well-known American doctor who founded the Preventive Medicine Research Institute, did some very interesting research on ageing and disease. He worked with Elizabeth Blackburn, one of the three American scientists who won the 2009 Nobel Prize in Physiology or Medicine for their study of telomeres, which are the body's markers of age. Telomerase enzymes increase the lifespan of our chromosomes and cells, which subsequently increase our overall lifespan. He did a test with ageing men with prostrate problems. After three months teaching them the importance of self-care by eating healthy, doing moderate exercise and relaxation techniques like yoga and meditation each day he saw a 30 per cent increase in their telomerase. Is this the elusive quest for longevity we have been looking for? Is it as simple as looking after ourselves holistically?

Research conducted in Ireland chiefly by Professor Rose Anne Kenny of Trinity College Dublin, known as TILDA (The Irish Longitudinal Study on Ageing), followed 9,000 adults for twelve years covering all aspects of life including sex, food, genetics and childhood experience, friendships and finance. The key findings to be as young as you feel were to: continually work on relationships and friendships; have a good laugh; de-stress daily; exercise; have a cold shower every morning; prepare for bed an hour beforehand; start yoga; eat within an eight-hour window. All of these were found to lead to a more positive attitude.

TIPS TO TRY

Start a checklist to see if you eat healthy five days a week, exercise for an hour three or four times a week, and have regular relaxation periods daily. While food and exercise are important, sleep is vital too. Prepare wisely by pottering around beforehand rather than browsing your phone or laptop in bed, as this is not conducive to the brain gently shutting down for a restful slumber. The more we look after our bodies, the easier it is to maintain good health and reap the benefits. This is not that hard to do and indeed to maintain but it does take consistency and effort.

WORDS OF WISDOM
Name: Gina Mackey.
Country of origin: Ireland.
Country of habitation: England.
Age: Fifty-six.
Occupation: Harpist and vocalist, wife and working mother of three girls.

1. What do you wish you had done or started earlier in your life?

I wish that I had studied music at university and got a music degree. This possibly would have given me a greater understanding and joy for my art and the gifts that I have been given. I started triathlon training at the age of forty-five and I can't believe it's taken me this long to discover the joys of open-water swimming in lakes.

2. What are you delighted you did or started earlier in your life?

I am delighted that I took the opportunity to travel around the world with my work when I was younger and without the responsibilities that I have now with family and home life. Sport and fitness was an important part of growing up and this now gives me a terrific sense of holistic well-being. I am thrilled to say my children have embraced this love of sporting activities as they grow up.

Chapter Three   OUR MAGNIFICENT BODIES

YOUR BODY IS YOUR HOME

Just like a snail with its shell, your soul is housed in your physical body. You alone have the responsibility to look after it. Not even the richest person in the world can pay someone to eat, sleep or exercise for them. This is such an intriguing thought. No matter how loving our parents, partners, children, friends or pets are, they cannot do it for us – this choice is ours.

REGULAR HEALTH CHECK-UPS

Before the age of fifty I didn't bother going to my doctor regularly, as I prided myself on the fact that I was in rude health and, therefore, assumed that there was no need to. Then it dawned on me that this was not a smart move. How would I know if there were any underlying issues until it was too late? So I went for a once-over with my local doctor where she assessed my physical body for all the usual ailments, including diabetes, precancerous cells, and heart issues. I pledged to do this every second year and in the intervening year I visit my dentist, optician and chiropodist. When time and money allow, I find it enjoyable and beneficial to treat myself to a massage or similar therapy that will give me an extra boost.

TIPS TO TRY
Make a folder where you file all your medical and health check-up information. This means that you readily have a means to view your progress over the years on subsequent appointments. Also make sure to let family members have easy access to this in case of an emergency. A bureau, drawer or shelf where you also store your financial information is often the best place.

THE WONDERS OF MEDICAL SCIENCE

I am a lover of all natural remedies but I view medical intervention as necessary and holistic therapies as complementary, not alternative. Both are of equal importance in any given situation. Over the years I have had the privilege to witness at close quarters the huge leaps we have made in how to treat the human body, both from new medical science and from the evolvement of ancient ways, especially in the field of energetic blockages. Think of hip and knee replacements, hidden hearing aids, chemotherapy and heart stents, as well as psychiatric care and bioenergy or shamanic treatments to name but a few. These are rapidly becoming mainstream here in the western world.

If you do need a medical procedure, and let's face it most of us will at some stage, then make sure that you trust and have faith in your doctor, surgeon and care team. You deserve the very best and so seek a second opinion if you feel the need to. Also remember that our medical and holistic practitioners deserve a patient that follows their sage advice, especially as regards aftercare such as physiotherapy and rest including taking any temporary or long-term medication.

There is, however, much we can do before we reach those stages by minding our precious health as best we can. Of course, our genetic pool comes into play plus wear and tear. If you do need an operation or treatment, especially of a serious illness, then recognise that your mental and emotional attitude can do much to help your medical and holistic team.

The old saying 'The food we eat and drink today walks and talks tomorrow' is true, so keep an eye on any overeating, junk-food binges and lolling about on the sofa too much.

A MYTH ABOUT ABDOMINAL SIZE

I have an interesting theory. Do you *ever* see healthy older women with flat abdomens, even if they have never had children? I have been fortunate to visit some indigenous people in far-flung places and even there with their lifestyles of strong physical work and no processed food, sugar or hydrogenated fat, both older men and women have 'a bit of a belly'. Could it be that the modern human is eternally on a quest for something that is impossible biologically unless we are sick? If at midlife we are yearning for the body we had in our twenties, is this as ridiculous as a teenager wanting the body of a child?

I have been blessed with a typical mesomorph body. In other words, an average body frame that if kept in regular, moderate exercise with a healthy diet would be a size ten becoming a twelve at menopause. At certain key times in my life, I had to make major adjustments. I discovered in my late twenties that I am intolerant to wheat and dairy. The former bloats me and the latter gives me sinusitis within twenty minutes. When I gave them up, I lost weight. The health of our body depends on how we feed and nourish ourselves on a daily basis; for example, reducing caffeine levels will help enormously with our ability to maintain a calm and relaxed demeanour. Coffee and black tea are morning drinks to perk us up for the day ahead. If we continue to imbibe these in the evening, our sleep will be affected. Three cups in the earlier part of the day is fine but any more and we are overstimulating our nervous system. As humans we are eating inordinate amounts of sugar in our food and any alcohol we drink. The amount of adult onset diabetes has rocketed in the western world due to this phenomenon. If we are mindful of the foods and drinks that contain higher levels of sugar and reduce our intake, this will hugely ameliorate many physical symptoms such as weight gain, anxious agitation and menopausal hot flushes.

As I approached midlife and became more aware of my energy levels through yoga, reiki and shamanic energy therapy, I found I couldn't tolerate many alcohols, including beer and wine. The hangovers were awful and my blood sugars dipped, which caused mood swings. I'm now down to minimal alcohol (sipping a gin with sparkling water or a good whiskey with ice) and have had to cut out all processed sugars. It was difficult to change old habits and took time to phase in, but the effect on my health was immediate and long lasting.

 TIPS TO TRY

If you think you are sensitive to any food types, then I highly recommend a simple food intolerance test. This can range anywhere from €60 to €500, depending on which foods and biomarkers are included. You can google the many options available to find a test that best matches your symptoms. A great source is the many local health food stores that will either offer this service or can recommend a local clinic that does. They also stock alternatives to wheat (spelt, oat crackers) and dairy (oat, soya, rice and almond milks), which are the classic intolerance foods. Don't worry – you will definitely not starve. It does take a bit of getting used to but is well worth the effort. The physical effects will be felt within a week, and the mental and emotional soon afterwords – hence the one-week cleanse in this book's appendix, which advocates a wheat, dairy and sugar-free regime to try out for yourself.

WISE EXERCISE

For fifteen years I taught yoga at home and abroad and as a holistic exercise it really kept me in shape physically, mentally, emotionally and spiritually. I don't teach classes anymore but I do practise every morning for ten minutes and attend classes locally four times a week. I walk daily now, whereas a few years ago I could get away with three times a week. It is important to be aware of your body and energy levels on any given day, and do only what you can. I was really impressed by Barack Obama when I watched footage of him on the campaign trail for the US presidential election. During his gym workout he picked up a set of weights. After trying them out, he put them down, saying that they were too heavy for him that day, and chose lighter ones – such honesty, humility and wisdom.

PREVENTION IS THE BEST MEDICINE

Our ears, knees and back are precious and necessary parts of our anatomy, and when we are young, we don't always appreciate just how much. I cringe when I think of the deafening music I repeatedly listened to, the high heels I tottered around in and the slouching posture I lounged about with. Did someone warn me or suggest I sit up straight or wear lower shoes? I am sure they did. But did I listen? Certainly not then but I have endeavoured to make up for lost time now.

Osteoarthritis, abbreviated to OA, is the most common form of arthritis, often referred to as degenerative joint disease or wear and tear arthritis. It occurs most frequently in the hands, hips and knees, causing stiffness and pain and sometimes swelling. It develops slowly and so may go unnoticed until it is too late to prevent any debilitating effects. OA may run in the family or be exacerbated by lifestyle choices; for example, if someone is very active and plays sport for most of their life then stops when they get older, their muscles, joints and bones will miss the activity and react to the lack of exercise, especially if there is an underlying condition. Plan to keep active and adapt when the time is right; for example, change your sport from football in your teens and twenties to five-a-side in your thirties and forties, to Zumba or golf in your fifties and bowls or aqua fit in your sixties and seventies and onwards.

TIPS TO TRY
When choosing exercise that is sustainable, it is so important to do something you like and enjoy. Walking and running are free and a great way to explore your locality, both solo to clear your head or with a friend to chat and socialise. You can also find inexpensive classes both locally and online to enjoy. There are many supermarkets and large retailers with low-cost exercise mats, blocks and bands.

Many men and women need a more endurance-based, physical-strength type of exercise. It can be very frustrating when you find it hard to keep up with the level of exercise you could do when you were younger and so run the risk of injury. Try to reach a balance between exercise that you aspire to and are capable of. If you recognise the importance of being in nature, then it makes sense to go for long walks in the fresh air. It might be worth investing in good all-weather outdoor clothing. Tune in to what works best for you and know that you are looking after yourself physically while enjoying a pursuit that makes your soul sing.

ROUTINE, ROUTINE, ROUTINE

I now have the classic mummy tummy without having given birth. I am postmenopausal and it felt like my body was cocooning itself as this life change occurred. For a few years I fretted over this and wished I were slimmer. I felt a bit ashamed and guilty because I espouse health and always prided myself on my figure, which to me was a badge of my healthiness. Then I woke up to the craziness of my aspirations, countering with positive self-talk along the lines of, 'You've got this, Karen. Just do the exercise you love, eat healthily all week and keep the treats to the weekend then get on with life.' So I began to follow this simple routine and I am delighted to say still do today.

What is the classic phrase? 'Change the things you can, accept the things you can't and have the wisdom to know the difference.' Our body is the first garment we put on and the last one we will ever wear. If we look after it, then we will be rewarded with good health. There is a fine line between not bothering to exercise and forcing yourself to do something that is not good for you. As we age our energy levels change, especially as we approach our sixties, so we need to adapt by changing what we do to suit our stage of life.

 WORDS OF WISDOM
Name: Carol Bermingham.
Country of origin and of habitation: Dublin, Ireland.
Age: Seventy-four.
Occupation: Shop assistant.
1. What do you wish you had done or started earlier in your life?
I wish I had learned to speak Irish. I would love to be able to talk in Irish and I would have loved to have learned how to drive.
2. What are you delighted you did or started earlier in your life?
That I had my children young and married young. We are married fifty-one years and are still happy.

MENOPAUSE
I think of menopause as a bit like being a teenager in reverse. Then we had spots and raging hormones. This time it's hot flushes and night sweats. Menopause is another time of transition. As with puberty, how we eat and exercise has a huge effect on how we sail or stumble through these times. Technically menopause is when we no longer menstruate each month due to a reduction in our levels of the hormones oestrogen and progesterone. It is a natural and inevitable stage of life and heralds the end of childbearing for women. Menopause doesn't happen overnight and usually occurs around fifty to fifty-three years of age. However, it may happen earlier. I started what is commonly called perimenopause at forty-six when my cycle started to become irregular, heavier

due to reduced progesterone, and I had slight hot flushes indicating that I was coming to the time of change in my cycle. During full menopause I had nightly sweats but I found that eating well, exercising regularly and looking after myself meant that it was not the scary concept that is often talked about.

For many women the symptoms of menopause can be severe and have a significant impact on day-to-day life. Those who experience menopausal symptoms that are troubling or those who experience symptoms before the age of forty-five should contact their GP for assistance. A doctor will assess your symptoms and recommend treatments and lifestyle changes to ease them. If necessary, a GP will refer you to a menopause specialist. There are treatments and support available to guide you through this stage of life, and it is important to reach out for help to find what is best for you.

There are also amazing books out there to help you pass through the menopause 'rite of passage' in the best way possible. I highly recommend Dr Christiane Northrup's *The Wisdom of Menopause* and my dear friend Paula Mee's *Your Middle Years* with her colleague Kate O'Brien.

There are two very important pieces of advice I can give you. Firstly, what you eat, what you drink and your level of stress will hugely inform how the symptoms are for you. I used to long for a way to be healthier and lose a few pounds and thought about how amazing it would be if I could achieve that easily or actually be motivated to do it continually. I found out through trial and error that my body was telling me in no uncertain terms that if I ate sugar and let my stress levels rise, I would have frequent and unpleasant hot flushes and night sweats. On the other hand, if I reduced the former and coped with the latter, they would significantly reduce. Trigger foods that will increase the unpleasant symptoms are sugar, alcohol (which is liquid sugar) and caffeine.

Secondly, talk about the menopause with your partner, family and friends frequently. Explain what is going on for you so they understand and can help or give you solace. Learn more and be positive. This is relevant if you still menstruate also; talk about that too. We need a sea change in our world to demystify this natural occurrence in half the world's population.

TIPS TO TRY
If you can clear your body and mind, it will help hugely as you pass through this time of transition in your life. A gentle cleanse (detox) is an enormous help if you are experiencing the early warning signs. I tend to prefer cleanses that involve regular healthy eating rather than those that cut everything out. (There is a sample in the appendix at the end of this book.) Hot flushes are a trial but they only last for two minutes or so. Wearing layers of clothes helps as you can just peel a cardigan or top layer off and cool down when you feel the flush about to start. Another great tip is to throw a leg or an arm out from under the duvet when a night sweat is coming on. A friend came to a great compromise with her partner: they now have two duvets on their bed, a warm one for him and a light one for her. They have great fun 'inviting' each other under their respective duvets for a cuddle and whatever!

HERBAL HELP
We are becoming more and more conscious of our planet, its health and how that affects our health. Whether it's the ozone layer, pollution or the decrease in fossil fuels, we are already making changes in our lives and homes with stronger sun creams, cloth shopping bags, water filters and the recycling of our waste. Many of us are shopping in the farmers markets that have set up all over our cities and towns, conscious of fresh produce that is so good for our physical bodies. As we move through this phase, is there anything else we can do to increase our health and longevity while looking after our body's hormones? Once again, Mother Nature herself (inexpensively) provides the answer.

Oestrogen acts as a gentle antidepressant so when levels deplete, we may be prone to feeling down. Some quiet time with slow, deep breathing helps lift low moods easily and organically. I'm a big fan of all things natural, and traditional herbal remedies really came into their own for me during my menopause. The classics from your local health food shops are:

- Black cohosh, in either tablet or tincture (liquid form), helps with hot flushes, low sexual drive, dry vagina, aches and pains, and mild depression.
- Sage, either in tablet or tincture form (from the leaves), is also great for hot flushes and night sweats. A sage herbal tea with a teaspoon of honey last thing at night is really helpful.
- Evening primrose, starflower or omega 3 oils really help reduce the pain associated with PMS (premenstrual syndrome) and menopause.
- Agnus castus assists with very frequent periods of heavy flow, fluid retention and breast soreness.
- Vitamin B6 helps to reduce anxiety, depression and irritability.

Your local health food shop will have a number of helpful information leaflets from the people who grow these organic plants and herbs and make the tinctures and tablets from them. You can read up on which is suitable for you to take at your leisure and make up your mind as to what is best for you. A natural and refreshing way to boost your immune system is to make your own herbal tea with a sprig of fresh thyme in boiled water. This wonderful herb has natural antimicrobial, antiviral and antifungal properties, the same as garlic but with a sweeter odour on your breath.

I supplemented the herbs I took with a multivitamin and mineral tablet. Naturally my body still let me know I was experiencing menopause, but certainly not in a dramatic way. It was also a fabulous reminder for me to clean up my act and cleanse while tweaking my eating and exercise habits to suit my age.

Menopause is not an illness; it is a natural phase of life during which we are changing and transforming on all levels. If we take the opportunity to celebrate and reinvent ourselves, if we avail of the wonderful herbs that empower us during this time, we can be stronger, sexier and more fabulous than ever!

THE MALE PERSPECTIVE
For husbands or partners, it can be very frustrating to feel sympathetic but ultimately not understand menopause in the same way that other women can. You might think that men get off lightly, with no physical symptoms in midlife. Anyone with prostate problems will tell you different. As with men and menopause, of course women will be sympathetic and encourage their partners to go to the doctor, but ultimately do not fully understand the male perspective. It is, therefore, important to talk to other men, who may have a better understanding or perhaps have experienced the same or similar issues themselves.

It is not common knowledge that men also feel mental and emotional effects at this age. Often their self-esteem is closely wrapped up in their career. In their forties they begin to notice the young bucks climbing up the ladder of promotion with, perhaps, new ideas and technologies unfamiliar to them. This is often an unsettling prospect to realise that they are no longer the kings of the castle or rate in quite the same way that they used to. This can cause a depressed feeling that may snowball if they have no one to talk to or if their primary relationship has deteriorated. Indeed, often the perceived threat comes from within – children who no longer take their father's word as worthy of respect. As with menopause, it is important to reach out for support and guidance to help make this transitionary time as easy on yourself as possible. Speak to your partner, your friends and, if necessary, your GP.

TIPS TO TRY
Saw palmetto is a plant tincture (from berries) that relieves
urinary discomfort, especially at night, if you have an
enlarged prostate gland. This gland sits near the bladder and
as men age it can enlarge, causing problems such as a feeling
of not completely emptying the bladder or weak urinary
flow. It is important to check with your doctor.

WORDS OF WISDOM
Name: Mícheál Ó Muircheartaigh.
Country of origin: Co. Kerry, Ireland.
Country of habitation: Co. Dublin from 1948–2006, now
Co. Meath.
Age: Ninety-one.
Occupation: Journalist and sports commentator.
**1. What do you wish you had done or started earlier in
your life?**
I wish I had directed sports associations to the duty of
maintenance of a healthy lifestyle for former players.
**2. What are you delighted you did or started earlier in
your life?**
I kept active and I travelled abroad and within Ireland. I
benefitted hugely from meeting different types of people
expressing views that were not mine. That was an education
as good as any university.

STAND TALL
Did you know that the earth's gravity eventually takes its toll
so that our height is lessened as we age? You may have noticed
that certain people who were known to be tall in their adult
life aren't any more now that they are older. Of course, our
daily posture has a big effect on us too. I invented a stretching
practice to do at bedtime that really makes a difference for
me. My husband thought it was hilarious at first but now he
sometimes uses this too for his quiet reflection time.

TIPS TO TRY

Place two pillows across your bed touching the edge. Lie over them, letting your head and neck hang off the bed for three to five minutes. You could use this time to say your prayers, to meditate or to give thanks for the day while reversing gravity's effect on your body. It feels really refreshing and is a lovely way to pause at the end of the day and reflect too. A good way to drift into sound sleep. Another tip is to pick something in your day that repeats regularly as a reminder to sit or stand up straight; for example, checking your phone messages, tweets or emails, making a cup of tea, getting in and out of the car. Once you get into the habit, it will become second nature to stretch and stand or sit up with a straight spine. The added advantage is that it is virtually impossible to be anxious or feel down when in a good posture. The reason is that now your natural energy is flowing throughout your whole body to elevate your mood.

Chapter Four   RELATIONSHIPS

HAPPY EVER AFTER

I used to think that when people fell out of love it was because they were incompatible from the start. Not necessarily so. I was shocked to discover that with no children, a relatively new marriage and an adoring husband, we hadn't made love in a week. Now you're probably laughing at this stage but I was perturbed. I had taken my eye off the proverbial ball, satisfied that my man loved me and I loved him and that was enough. Of course, at the time it was but how long do you think before it wasn't? Nothing was wrong in our relationship, in fact quite the contrary, but we had so much going on in our lives that we lost the time and opportunities for intimacy. Now imagine if we had four children, an aged parent to look after plus two jobs in a difficult economic climate: see where this could head? Frequently people come into my clinic and are honest enough to admit that this is exactly the case with them. Life gets in the way and we become wrapped up in our busy world trying to provide the material comforts we think we need. Sometimes we forget that children would much prefer happy, loving parents with respect for each other than the extra material possessions that overtime provides.

Empty nest syndrome is when couples reach a stage in life where their children have grown and left the family home, and the parents are rattling around a house that used to be full of noise and busyness. Imagine how much more difficult this would be if you looked at your partner and didn't know who they were anymore. 'I remember I used to love you once' can be quite a common refrain among older couples. Many drift into what used to be called 'divorce Irish style' – a couple living together, sharing a bed but not talking intimately or making love anymore.

A woman once told me that she discovered a whole new aspect to her marriage when she asked her husband to support her fitness efforts by walking with her in the local park every evening. She said it was the makings of their long-term future relationship as they confided in each other in a way they had never done before. She put much of this down to the fact that they were watching where they were walking and so could open up in a more honest way without looking each other in the eye.

 TIPS TO TRY
We need to find the time and energy to put into our relationships on a daily and weekly basis. Do you ever watch two different screens in two different rooms or eat a meal in silence while sinking into complacency? Then switch it up! Take the time and space to be together and share a joke, laugh or play. This could be suggesting to your partner that you take out a pack of cards, watch a comedy together or start a hobby. Make it a temporary pursuit initially to see if you both like it and subsequently see if it grows into something longer term. This could be the difference between merely existing together and a sense of fulfilling happiness.

PERSONAL DEVELOPMENT

If one person in a relationship develops themselves but their partner stagnates, then no matter how much they love each other, problems will occur as time goes on and the differences become apparent. We are not to know when we fall in love that one of us will continually work on ourselves, ironing out life's problems and sorting out anything that needs to be looked at, and the other will not. Perhaps this is something that needs to be discussed at the premarital/pre-partner stage. Subconsciously we learn about being in relationship by watching how our parents are in theirs. If they continually develop as they move through the various stages of life, then we have a blueprint for how we can be in relationship. If they didn't, however, then no need to worry unnecessarily. The good news is that we can learn how to do this of our own volition at any stage in life. All we need to be is aware of what is not working and figure out how to turn it around.

It is relatively easy to leave personal development out of the mix of life skills. Many people don't realise how important it is. We can't simply meander through life without learning from our mistakes and adjusting how we behave because of them. Yet huge numbers of us do think that it is enough to live from day to day never questioning how our behaviour affects others and blaming them if life isn't working out exactly as we planned. Have you ever wondered why you are angry or frustrated or sad and taken responsibility for your part in it? This is a huge insight that many of us aren't ever taught about formally.

A couple, married nearly seven years, came to see me as they felt their marriage was over and they wanted help to tie up the loose ends. After one session it became obvious that they had assumed that because they were not happy they would have to end their marriage and move on. It never occurred to them to sit down and figure out what had actually gone wrong so they could try and adjust their behaviour and rekindle their love for each other. In their marriage vows they had said a version of 'for better, for worse, in sickness and in health' but they hadn't really taken on board what that meant. They honestly thought that all couples that 'survived' their relationships to old age were either putting up with each other or somehow had the magic wand for relationships. As if! I explained about the power of honest communication, compassion and honouring the soul of their partner. As a counselling psychotherapist, however, I fully understand that sometimes a partnership does run its course and parting amicably is what is best for all.

TIPS TO TRY
To develop ourselves personally, every so often we need to take a good hard look at who we have become. Do we actually like ourselves? Have we copied a parent and are acting just like them, including their faults? Do we look at how our actions are perceived by others, especially our loved ones? Are you always late? Do you continually skip buying the first round of drinks as it is usually the most expensive? Do you forget birthdays? How is your personal hygiene? Can you change this behaviour for the better and observe the reactions of your family and friends? It can reveal a lot about you if you are able to magnanimously admit that you were remiss and accept that this is now a new way to be. A true test with small children is to ask them to play the Mummy and Daddy roles. They will show you clearly what they see you both do and say on a regular basis. This can be very illuminating. You could also ask a trusted friend if there is anything you need to look at.

THE TRUTH CAN HURT, YET HELP AND HEAL

During one such conversation a friend told me that I had the habit of starting sentences with 'No, but'. I genuinely had no idea of this irritating habit. Basically, I was listening to others, disagreeing with them in my mind and coming up with alternatives; so, when I said 'No, but' what I was really saying was 'I don't agree with your idea, mine is much better'. Because I had actually listened to them, I thought I was being polite. I now try to start sentences with the word 'yes' and I back off trying to fix every situation with my way of doing things. What a gift that friend gave to me in offering an important warning to change my ways.

PROJECTIONS AND COMMUNICATION

I frequently work with women and men who ask me what to do when there is a row brewing or something sensitive they need to communicate with their partner. I suggest they take some quiet time to figure out what they really want to say. This is also an opportunity to own any projections they may have towards their significant other. In other words, are they projecting their own thinking onto someone else? Perhaps they are assuming that the other person is feeling X or Y, or even reacting like their own mother or father did. This is a fairly frequent occurrence for many.

TIPS TO TRY

If you have ever been in a situation like this, then after a reflection period pick a particular time to talk to your partner. Wait until they are fed, rested, relaxed and in a good mood. Then approach them and suggest that you would like to talk about something that is bothering you. This shows them that it is a serious discussion, yet you are owning your feelings straight away. Too often people start this type of conversation with 'You did this' or 'I hate it when you'. The consequence of this is usually a defensive reaction from the person on the receiving end. Not a great start to any type of effective communication.

Calmly state what is going on for you by phrasing each sentence in the style of 'when this happens, I feel', so you are acknowledging your own feelings but not blaming them, while also pointing out what you perceive needs to change. This way you are stating clearly why you feel the way you do and what you think the cause is. Finally, ask the other person to help you come up with a solution. This last piece is very important. How are we going to implement something that we haven't actually devised? Perhaps there is a better solution that you haven't given your partner a chance to suggest. At this stage some of my clients ask, 'Why am I the one to have to work around their moods?' This is a very good question. The answer is because *you* want something to change and are now simply setting the scene for the best way to achieve this for both of you. Honest communication with ourselves and our partners is the key.

MATURE LOVE

We hear so much about first love – that delicious honeymoon phase when we connect with another soul at a deep loving level. There is a plethora of music, poetry and prose about the feelings and sensations of this gorgeous human experience. Even though many of us try valiantly to extend and hold onto it, there is a finite time to this very beautiful stage in our lives. We are in such a wonderfully altered state, focused on our love and giddy with the excitement of it all. However, this euphoric feeling is unsustainable beyond a few weeks or months since it is so intense. I am amazed that we don't really hear about something very different but to me equally delightful and long term – mature love. You know that fabulous feeling when we know our partner so well that we can start and finish each other's sentences? When we are at a party and a smile across the room speaks volumes, or we kiss passing each other on the stairs, laundry in hand, or when chasing a recalcitrant child up to bed there's a 'promise' for later in our quick glance! This phase is very special and needs to be honoured by both partners as well as fuelled by time and energy to maintain its magic.

DIFFERENT TYPES OF LOVE

Love makes the world go around and there are many forms of it. The obvious ones are marriage or life partnership and love of our parents and children. Not all of us are in relationships or have offspring, and so other forms of love that are equally important may feature more prominently in later life. These include love in strong friendships, of our cherished pets and Mother Nature herself. For everyone the most important and difficult of all is self-love, and that may take an entire lifetime to master. How we love may differ from person to person; it doesn't matter as long as you know you experience it. That is fundamental to a happy life.

WORDS OF WISDOM

Name: B. Spitzer.

Country of origin: America.

Country of habitation: Ireland.

Age: Eighty-one.

Occupation: Nurse and homemaker.

1. What do you wish you had done or started earlier in your life?

Spent less time working and more with the family and home. Had more children when young, living in the present moment to focus on gratitude for what I had.

2. What are you delighted you did or started earlier in your life?

Enjoyed time in the countryside and resort places, my interest in decorating our homes and gardens, our pets to care for and enjoy. Now I am healthy enough to see my grandchildren grow.

RELATIONSHIP ISSUES

During my career as a counselling psychotherapist, I have listened to many individuals and couples with relationship problems. I have been privileged to work with them on reconnecting and continuing their relationship better than ever or breaking up amicably. In an ideal world we would be with the same partner for life but it doesn't always work out like that. If you do reach a point where you wonder should you leave or stay, then perhaps the following options might be of interest to consider.

TIPS TO TRY

1. You could try to work out the problem to see if the relationship might still be viable. If you do leave and meet up with a new partner and you haven't changed anything about yourself or the triggers you react to, there is a strong eventuality that the same problem will reappear.

2. You could still leave but work on the problems so they don't reoccur. This could also help to retain a friendship with your ex-partner. An amicable split is particularly valuable when there are children involved.

3. You could leave wanting freedom, space and another relationship, but miss the family home and lifestyle. This is a consideration I have found many people do not think of. They know the relationship is not working for them and may seek to replace that outside of the partnership. However, frequently the one who leaves is shocked to discover that they really miss the family home and the life that their ex-partner created for them all. The full implications of their new existence only begin to dawn on them when it is too late. Therefore, an amicable split or another attempt to resolve issues is a wise move before you make your final decision, ideally together.

THE SEVEN-YEAR ITCH

Do you remember the fabulous film of that title with Marilyn Monroe? The premise is that every seven years we get itchy feet in our relationship and start to look elsewhere. I really think there is something to this but in a different way than you might think. Scientists reckon that every seven years each cell in our body has been replaced by replicas of the originals. Doesn't it make sense that our minds and emotions might be changing too?

TIPS TO TRY

The seven-year mark might be a timely reminder to jazz things up, shake off any complacency and spice up your love life. Even if nothing apparent is wrong, a change is as good as a rest. It keeps a sense of progression and movement in your relationship. Happy ever after takes time, energy and commitment. So, book that exotic holiday, take up an exciting hobby or plan a change together.

FAMILIES

In the 1970s there were two American television programmes that depicted family life: *The Waltons* and *Little House on the Prairie*. Most of the characters got on extremely well together. Is this possible in real life? Can we click equally well with our mother, father and all our siblings? I believe that is not always the case. It's fine to admit you don't get on as well with your sister as your brother or are a daddy's girl or mummy's boy or vice versa. In fact, it is very possible to not like a family member yet love them and be there for them in times of need.

TIPS TO TRY

Did you ever catch yourself sounding like your mother or father saying something in the same tone of voice they used? Scary, isn't it? Especially when it is not something that you ever thought you would want to say – a reprimand or order of some kind. We can choose to be different and bring the best of our original family's habits with us into our new family life. If anything clearly didn't work, then choose to leave it behind consciously. Make a point of trying new ways of saying things – your way. It takes six weeks to make a habit and six weeks to break one, so persevere and soon you will be delighted to parent or partner in your own unique style.

FAMILY STRUCTURES AGE TOO

When your parents age, their role within the family changes and this will cause ripples throughout the whole structure. Imagine the mother and father role as the lynchpin holding the family dynamic together. Ideally, they provide support, nurture and protection for everyone in the early years of their children's development. In theory they teach their daughters and sons to replicate this role in their future families. If for some reason this life lesson has not been taught as the children grow up, then some unpleasant scenarios may unfold:

- The parents don't relinquish their role and continue to mother or father their adult children, interfering in their relationships and parenting.
- The parents do naturally relinquish their role but needy adult children don't want them to and react badly, blaming them for all their woes, not taking responsibility for their own lives.

TIPS TO TRY

If this sounds all too familiar, please note that awareness goes a long way to resolving the problem. Usually, it can be sorted relatively easily. If you are the parent, then pull back slowly from your adult children's lives. More than likely any son- or daughter-in-law has been reacting negatively if you are too involved in their partner's life. This is a telling sign that you need to let go of your parenting role and allow your children to lead their own life and indeed make their own mistakes. If you are the adult child still attached to your parents, then strike out on your own. If you take the risk, you will reap the benefits in personal empowerment and self-responsibility.

FRIENDSHIPS

Our friendships are relationships too. They can be deep and meaningful lifelong experiences or of the fleeting fair-weather variety. As our lives change so will our friendships, either morphing along as we change or staying stagnant and so falling by the wayside. We hear lots of talk about meeting new people and starting friendships, but nobody really shares how they end when they pass their sell-by date. People do grow apart, move on and acquire different interests. That's life. Ever moved into a distinctly new phase of your life and recognised that some of your friends haven't moved with you? Usually it is after leaving school, college or a job, getting married or having a baby. Your focus and environment have changed but your friends haven't necessarily changed theirs. Of course, if there is a deep connection of friendship then they will flow along with you. I really believe that if we have a handful of lifelong friends, we are very lucky indeed. There is a wonderful phrase to do with friendships referred to as 'a time and a place', meaning that at a certain time and in a certain place you can have a fantastic friendship; however, it is important to know that once that time and place no longer exist, it is fine to retain the fond memories and move on with no regrets.

Then there are the 'duty' friendships. Perhaps for one of you the friendship is over but you feel you have to stay in touch. Maybe the other person expects you to be their friend even though you have nothing in common anymore. This can be difficult especially if one of you is a godparent or has been a bridesmaid or best man, so there is history to your friendship. I know someone who does what he calls a 'friendship test' every year. For a few weeks he doesn't phone any friends to see if they will contact him. If they don't, he might wait a bit longer. Then he feels that he can let them go, think fondly of them but know that the time and place have changed and it is appropriate to gently let the friendship fall away naturally.

TIPS TO TRY
We need to acknowledge that as we grow older our
priorities change and we may have less energy for a big
group of acquaintances. We need a fine balance between
making the effort and staying in touch. Most times these
friendships will just slip away naturally but sometimes it
may take an honest heart-to-heart chat. Here's a simple tip
whenever you meet an old acquaintance and are not sure
how to finish the brief chat. You can avoid doing the old 'we
must meet for lunch' routine that adds to your never-ending
to-do list. Instead, say genuinely, 'It was great to bump into
you and catch up. Hopefully we'll meet again sometime.'
Then you have caught up on old times but with no sense of
prolonging what is past.

ADOLESCENT RELATIONSHIPS

In my clinic I see some gay and lesbian clients who knew as a
child that their sexual preference was different from some of
their peers. Most people presume that this would occur at
puberty, but time and time again they share that they knew
at seven and eight years of age, sometimes even younger. I
also noted that my nieces and nephews around the same
age began to take interest in each other's expression of self.
Then at puberty there is an advancement of this interest into
action. I listened to a couple of fourteen-year-olds discuss
their *ceili* partners and would they 'go out' with them if
asked. One young girl said shyly yet quite confidently that
she wasn't ready yet and would wait until she felt she was.
How amazing is that? My point is that adults – whether
parents, aunts, uncles, godparents or grandparents – need
to talk to young people about relationships. Tell them what
to be aware of, what mistakes we made. As a young girl, I
often panicked when asked out by a boy. My first thought
was how to get rid of him if it didn't work out. I literally didn't
know what to do as I was too embarrassed to ask my parents.
My friends didn't know either and I was too young to know

what to say so I would ignore the poor chap and refuse to answer his calls. The torment we must have caused these poor brave lads.

TIPS TO TRY
It is actually quite easy to say no in a nice way. The old 'thank you but no thank you' works every time. It lets someone know how you feel but also allows them to save face and retain their dignity. Talk to any teenagers you know about how to do this. Mention sexual identity in a casual way too in case any of them might be LGBTQ+. Let them know that they or their friends can talk to you about this if they need to. If you feel too embarrassed to broach the subject, then make sure that someone who can talk to them does.

WORDS OF WISDOM
Name: Kathleen Quinn.
Country of origin: USA.
Country of habitation: Canada.
Age: Seventy.
Occupation: Social justice advocate, charitable sector.
1. What do you wish you had done or started earlier in your life?
I graduated in linguistics and learned a little bit of several languages, including Irish Gaelic. I wish I had become proficient in a second language. I am now focusing on increasing my knowledge of Irish and I think I will also study Cree, to honour the Indigenous people in the land where I live.
2. What are you delighted you did or started earlier in your life?
In 1985, a group of women in Edmonton, Alberta, Canada, watched a film called *Behind the Veil*. This film opened our eyes and hearts to the spirit of Brigid. Since then I have continued to honour her presence in my life, through small

group gatherings, workshops, rituals and pilgrimage walks, both here in Edmonton and in Ireland. Pure delight! On 11 April 2020 I joined the Brigid's Way Celtic Pilgrimage FireKeepers with their innovative 'Brigid in the Backyard' response to the pandemic when people in Ireland had to stay within two kilometres of their home. I walked around our neighbourhood to spread Brigid's cloak of protection. The next weekend my husband joined me. We are still walking.

NEW MATURE ROMANCES

We are living so much longer than our ancestors so the idea of a second career is not new. However, the concept of a second romance after a long-term marriage may seem like a step too far. I am not talking about anyone in their forties or younger who, like me and my peers, have had a variety of romantic liaisons before commitment to a long-term partnership. I am referring to anyone in their sixties, seventies and eighties who may have had only one life partner who has now gone or passed away. I fully respect that some may have been with their soulmate for years and that has been more than enough for this lifetime. I am aware from my clinic work that some were in restrictive relationships and are never going to give up newly found freedom again. Fair enough. Yet I have come across a lot of clients that are lonely and would like to consider a new relationship but don't know where to start. One woman has false teeth and that has held her back from even contemplating the next step. I counsel that it really is a bit like going back to your teenage dating years, but this time with wisdom!

TIPS TO TRY
Acknowledge your open but naturally protected heart – like a beautiful rose with thorns. If you have unfinished business grieving for your previous partner,

then you must do this first. No point going into a new liaison with old baggage to sort out. Next, check out facilities in your area that are conducive to meeting new people in and around your age and circumstances; for example, a ballroom dancing class, a theatre or book club. Brush up your look with some new clothes and/or accessories and off you go. I recommend arranging to meet someone you know even vaguely there to break the ice the first time or tell the organiser you are a bit shy so they will make sure to introduce you to everyone when you arrive.

Chapter Five   CHOICES

WHAT DO WOMEN REALLY WANT?
This is a question that men have asked for millennia and deep down the answer is always the same. Women want the ability to choose. Smart men know that the way to a woman's heart is to consult with her, offering choices from the profound to the mundane. Then she is truly equal but different, having been rated, considered and conferred with. Naturally women offer this same respectful phenomenon back to their menfolk, but in the patriarchal society that has existed for millennia, and indeed still does exist, this option is key to true equality and harmony.

FERTILITY
If having a say is a huge part of a woman's life, then it makes sense that when she no longer has a choice in her ability to reproduce, there will be feelings and emotions that reflect this circumstance. Her natural right as a woman has now changed and she has clearly entered a new phase. Many women with children find it paradoxical that they mourn this change of life when they have beautiful children that they love and, in truth, know that they don't yearn for any more. It is the lack of choice that they truly miss, the 'I could if I wanted to' decision. I experienced this – one of the biggest changes that heralds growing old for a woman – in my mid-forties. I always knew the day would come but there was an extra

tinge of sadness to this for me since we weren't blessed with children. Biologically, it's not the same for men. Of course, they miss the fact that their wife or partner no longer has the choice to procreate for both of them but their choices end in a different way. More about this important topic later on.

TIPS TO TRY
Take some time out to soul-search on how you are about the loss of choice around your fertility or indeed any phase of life that has passed by. If you think about it and feel fine, then that is a good sign that you have naturally worked through and managed this issue. If you find yourself becoming upset or feeling angry, then that is a sure indicator that some work needs to be done to process these emotions. Often simply owning and releasing these emotions will work. The merits of a good cry are well known. Sometimes talking it over with your partner or good friend will be all you need. If these feelings persist, then seek professional help such as through the Irish Association of Counselling and Psychotherapy (www.iacp.ie), of which I am proud to be a member.

EMPTY NEST SYNDROME
Empty nest syndrome is well documented as a phenomenon and we mentioned this earlier when discussing relationships. Now we will dig a little deeper. Mothers may feel an almost visceral ache as their 'babies' leave the nest. Fathers often miss the noise and community of their family about the house. How one copes depends on the relationship between the two parents once the grown-up children have left.

In Ireland there is a shift towards a complete reverse situation where the adult children either can't or don't leave the nest. This can cause huge problems not just for the frustrated parents but for the stunted growth of the 'full nesters'. The economic climate has a lot to do with it but also the fact that many homes are, in fact, the best 'free hotels' and so why would adult children want to leave? There are some parents who may not actually want them to go as it would show up cracks in their own relationship. If the young adults don't go risking all the usual ups and downs of fending for themselves, then there is a break in the chain of natural growth as an adult. If they don't leave home of their own free will, then in a relatively short space of time they may end up minding their aged parents, which, while being a wonderful thing to do, leaves a gap in their personal growth that can lead to bitterness and resentment.

PERCEPTIONS OF CHOICE

The choices we perceive we can no longer make may not actually be real. Sometimes we limit ourselves through our own lack of imagination or understanding. I know a great-granny who spent a lot of frustrating hours coming to grips with texting as she knew that the only way she could easily keep in touch with her grandchildren was to communicate like them. She laughs when she imagines what she will have to learn next as her very young great-grandchild grows up! I remember when my husband bought us our first fancy smartphones and I have to confess to flinging mine across the desk in frustration, as I couldn't do the most basic tasks. Patient hubby came to the rescue, teaching me a new feature every day until I got the hang of it. Eventually it was a friend who converted me completely, by showing me how to check the weather worldwide at the flick of a few buttons. Curiosity won the day in the end and I began to love my new gadget.

In 2012 I decided to go back to college to do a masters, followed by a doctorate. This idea had been with me for a long time and I sat with the reason why for a few years. Did I want to do it for the love and glory of having a few letters before and after my name? Was I trying to impress anyone? Did I feel at this stage of my career that a new status would open extra doors for me? Friends and family thought I was mad. Did I have any idea of the time and effort it would take to do? Study was something you did in your youth, not as you grew older. Yet the idea wouldn't go away. I was the type of kid who looked forward to going back to school every September. I loved the summer holidays but I liked academia too. I wanted to learn more, to challenge myself and in the case of these further studies link my counselling psychotherapy skills with my beloved energy therapy work. It took me seven long, hard years to become Dr Karen Ward MA as I chose to study part time while continuing to run my clinic and co-direct our school of Irish Celtic Shamanism. I really had to push myself in new directions with the technical side of research online, which initially was a nightmare for me – a proverbial dinosaur compared to my young peers. Yet I thoroughly enjoyed many of the tasks I needed to complete to further my education, especially stimulating my brain as well as bringing my experience of clinic work to a different level. Meeting wonderful fellow students and colleagues of all ages during our exciting coffee conversations was a huge bonus.

 TIPS TO TRY

Is there anything you yearn to do but are limiting yourself through lack of imagination or self-confidence? More study opportunities? Weight loss or a new look? A new skill? Take the time to write a wish list or bucket list of things you'd really love to do. They can be fairly routine, feats of daring, whims and fancies or lifelong ambitions – whatever takes your fancy. Now have a good, hard look and see if there is a way to make them happen now. Ask 'Mrs Google' and see what is offered in your locality. Start a discussion with friends and family who might be very happy to accompany you to the class or minibreak or contribute to your plans in some helpful way.

I find a great way to make some wish list items a reality is to morph them into hobbies, holidays or make a deadline. For example, I always wanted to enhance my craftwork and creative skills, so I took up photography as a hobby and went to a stitch-and-bitch class where a group of women knit and gossip together. I fancied going to Machu Picchu so I did a charity trek there initially and subsequently led three groups to this sacred site with John, my husband, over many years. I wanted to learn to sing Irish songs so I decided to learn a few for a trip to the US where the friends we visited were into performing party pieces around a campfire.

 WORDS OF WISDOM
Name: Paddy Whitty.
Country of origin: Kildare/Dublin, Ireland.
County of habitation: Cobh, Co. Cork.
Age: Seventy-nine.
Occupation: Irish army radio/radar technician, Irish naval chief petty officer, lieutenant commander naval logistics, husband of wonderful Ann, father of four beautiful daughters, retiree, Cobh town councillor and mayor of Cobh twice.

1. What do you wish you had done or started earlier in your life?
While I am not the type to look back and wonder what might have been, I think leaving school at the intermediate certificate stage was a mistake; however, I can safely claim to have made up for that later and definitely have no regrets. While I am proud of my academic record, holding down a full-time job and pursuing studies at night while my children were still school-going, in retrospect, it may not have been very fair to them.

2. What are you delighted you did or started earlier in your life?
We were married when we were both young, and consequently are now very active grandparents with the energy to enjoy our seven lovely grandchildren and two great-grandchildren, while also availing of every opportunity to travel the world now that we have an empty nest.

LEARNING TO SAY NO

I love musicals; so jolly, lively and dramatic. I learn a lot from their upbeat, can-do messages. One that particularly comes to mind is the title of a song from *Oklahoma!* called 'I'm Just a Girl Who Can't Say No'. The character in the musical was singing about romantic situations but I think the message can be transferred to a way of being for many of us today. We may have in our early days said yes to a range of people for a variety of reasons; to our parents and teachers as our elders, or our bosses and managers in work, or our friends and partners for approval and affection. Now we are grown adults in the latter half of our lives with more time but less energy. If we keep saying yes to everything and everyone, we'll soon be exhausted and possibly resentful.

The late Paul Newman, fine actor and Hollywood heart-throb, was a great example. He had saying no down to a fine art. It was a case of having to since he was constantly mobbed with requests for autographs. He would smile with his twinkly blue eyes and say, 'Thank you so much but I don't do autographs.' The asker went away without an autograph but with their dignity and pride intact since he talked to them with respect and kindness.

TIPS TO TRY

There are different phases of our lives when it is appropriate and important to say yes, but as we age and change we have a choice. Saying no gracefully is an art, a bit like delegating. Some are naturally better than others but we can *all* learn how to do it. Firstly, buy time with sentences like, 'Thank you very much for asking me, can I get back to you later?' Now you have some time to think of the implications of your answer.

The secret is to be firm but kind. If you feel you are saying yes to everyone because after a lifetime of saying yes they now expect you to, then be aware that when you change this habit there will be a ripple effect. People will be surprised and even disappointed and perhaps angry or frustrated. That is fine. They'll get over it. Stick to your principles and be clear. Don't give mixed messages by giving in after a while. When you decide to say no then you must stick to it.

 WORDS OF WISDOM
Name: Valia Carmenate Fernández.
Country of origin and habitation: Cuba, but I lived in Mexico for many years.
Age: Fifty-eight.
Occupation: Therapist and reiki teacher.
1. What do you wish you had done or started earlier in your life?
Now I know that everything I lived and did in my life was the best. Although I feel content, there was a dream I held for many years but I did not follow, and that was practising rhythmic gymnastics. I had all possibilities to grow in that field, but circumstances were not ideal. It took me many years to accept it.
2. What are you delighted you did or started earlier in your life?
I look back to the path travelled and I am proud I took the decision and had the courage to leave behind the safety of the place I was born and raised in. I went in search of the unknown to a new place from where I started my spiritual journey and began to understand my existence.

CHOICES OPENING UP
When I was growing up travel meant going on an annual holiday with the whole family to another county in Ireland. Those who were lucky enough to go on a continental trip were unusual and often envied. Nowadays taking a plane to a foreign clime is commonplace and might happen a few times a year, though we are all becoming more environmentally conscious now. This can open a whole new world as we get older. We have the time, the money and the lack of responsibility for

childminding and onerous work commitments. All the exotic places we may have dreamed of when we were young can now become a reality. I know a woman who wanted to travel but was frightened of the prospect of going alone. Would she be a target for muggers, unwelcome romantics or sad lonely people with no friends? She laughs now having discovered the joys of fancy package deals to rugby matches, operas and painting holidays in Europe. She feels safe, protected and in the good company of like-minded retirees her own age. She's going off on a yoga trip next and is seriously considering walking the pilgrim route of the Santiago de Compostela over the Pyrenees into north Spain.

I love the idea of updating myself every so often. I used to do that when I worked abroad. In the flight on the way over I'd make quantum leaps in ways of being; for example, trying out some newly won confidence, a recent skill or highlighting a particular interest that I might not have had time for in the old rut at home. Then when I eventually returned home, I'd bring these innovative ways with me, sometimes to the delight and amazement of family and friends. I developed a love of photography during my years in London, camping when in Texas and singing in France.

 TIPS TO TRY

Why not consider the idea of renewing yourself? What could you do first? Would it be a more confident approach to an existing situation? Perhaps a new hobby or interest? A creative means to express yourself? Maybe getting a pet if you have never had one or not since childhood. This might be the exact time to make some positive changes based on your greatest dreams. The saying that 'it's now or never' is true. What are we waiting for? Life is too short and we can seize the day by creating fabulous opportunities for exciting experiences. It is important to be realistic, though, as some things may become less feasible or less attractive with the wisdom of age. I always fancied the idea of going to a Grand

Prix; however, now the noise and the pollution do not appeal to my environmental sensitivities – or my ears.

DESTINY

I believe that we are all born to fulfil our destiny, to find our true path in life. This is distinct from fate, which is what happens to us as we muddle along. We might start by going to the school we are sent to, taking the job someone arranged for us, marrying the boy or girl next door and eventually living life through our children. Then one day we wake up and think 'Who am I? Have I got a say in what I do?' Yes, of course you have but you'd better do it sooner rather than later. It's never too late and any time is infinitely better than doing nothing but thinking about it.

A friend of mine told me an interesting story. She knew a very talented man who always talked about writing a book. He was a journalist and had a fascinating life full of exciting assignments and travel. Recently she attended his funeral, where so many people said that they really wished he had written what would clearly have been a thoroughly good read detailing his many amazing experiences. Unfortunately, with the busyness of life he never got around to writing his memoir and now it was too late.

Chapter Six   SOCIETY'S VIEW OF OLD AGE

PHASES OF OUR LIFE
The Druids who lived on these Celtic Isles many moons ago
understood that we had three very distinct phases of our life.
For women it was the maiden or young girl phase, then the
mother phase and finally the crone or wise woman phase. For
men it was the boy, the father and the sage or wise man. Each
of these stages of life varied slightly from person to person,
in much the same way as a baby usually walks in or around
one year of age. The maiden phase ended in those days when
the young woman began to reproduce or partnered sexually
for the first time and became a mother. The boy moved into
his father phase when he gained his apprenticeship, took a
partner or became a father. The woman changed from her
mother role at menopause and moved into her wise woman
or crone role. The man changed from his father role when his
children left home and he relinquished his work role in the
tribe to a younger man and became a wise man or sage.

There were very distinct rites of passage at each of these
phases. Many of them fell every seven years, as scientifically
every cell in our body has been renewed at least once every
seven years, so we start anew. Depending on where you live
and your religious upbringing, the modern equivalent would
be a first holy communion, which used to be age seven, a
confirmation or bar or bat mitzvah at fourteen, a twenty-first
birthday party or ending of apprenticeship time, a wedding or

partnering ceremony or birth of children at around twenty-eight, and so on until retirement at sixty-three years of age.

The beauty of these distinct times in our lives was that it allowed us to acclimatise to growing older in ways that were honoured and had been mapped by previous generations. We didn't find ourselves floundering physically, mentally, emotionally or spiritually at any stage but had help in the form of older loved ones or societal role models on how to prepare to move from phase to phase. I found the approach to menopause, called perimenopause, a strange time as I had no reference for it at all. The women in our family did not talk about these things. I wasn't ready to be a crone or older woman, yet my body was telling me in no uncertain terms that I was moving into a new stage of life. I felt like a tweenie, a gawky young girl in between a child and a teenager; a bit like Bambi walking on spindly legs.

HOMEMADE RITES OF PASSAGE

If you are not part of a particular religious following and feel the need for some way of moving from one stage of life to another, then you can create your own ceremonial celebration. I have had the honour of facilitating baby-naming ceremonies, becoming-a-teenager parties and handfasting marriages in a spiritual but non-denominational way. These people recognised the need to acknowledge important life phases in their own way with a personal form of spirituality, witnessed by family and friends. Not surprisingly the elements that comprise these events are quite similar to more formal religious ceremonies, the main difference being the personal input and freedom of form.

TIPS TO TRY

Imagine you were to invent a special way to mark getting older. What would you do and who would witness it? For example, you might have a special birthday party or go on a long-dreamed-of trip abroad to visit an iconic site such as Machu Picchu or somewhere fun like Las Vegas. Perhaps you might do something that is a challenge such as paragliding or a charity walk. Maybe you could look back on certain stages in your life and acknowledge the importance of the celebrations that took place then, whether they were formal or not.

Part of my personal wish list is to walk the Dublin City Marathon in under six hours and to see the aurora borealis – the Northern Lights in Scandinavia – as I prepare to celebrate my 'crone-hood' when I reach sixty. Then I might have a party, renew my wedding vows and do something private with my close girlfriends. So far that feels right to do. I don't intend to retire from my career as, to be honest, it is my life's vocation, my passion and who I am. I imagine that will change and evolve as I grow but still within the sphere of holistic health.

HOW TO BE A WISE ELDER

I'd like to be an example to younger women on how to be a successful older woman so that instead of fearing it or avoiding it they might embrace the opportunities it brings. Many people that I know have had a wonderful, even if brief, experience of time with their grandparents. Perhaps you have heard the expression 'You're at your granny's' when someone feels very comfortable in any given situation. The idea being that you could do things at your grandmother's house that your parents would never let you get away with. The reason, of course, is that most parents are busy trying to hold down jobs, pay mortgages, cope with all the vicissitudes of life, while grandparents may be more relaxed and have more time. They tend to be a bit more lenient too since they don't have to babysit 24/7. In indigenous societies like the Aborigines, the Native Americans and the Maoris, the grandparents had and still have a big role to play officially in the rites of passage for children and teenagers. They not only had more time than parents, but also had vital wisdom and life experience to pass on.

TIPS TO TRY

Grandparents often teach young children special life lessons such as knitting, fishing, tying laces and baking. They often observe things that busy parents might miss, like a child being bullied or not adjusting to a new school. Children may try to hide these things from stressed parents but grandad's beady eye misses nothing. What do you remember from time spent with your grandparents or any older relatives? If you have grandchildren, have you had the opportunity to teach them anything? Have a little brainstorm about what you could do with them in the future.

EMBRACING OUR NATURAL ELDER BEAUTY

I'd like to think we can gain a new appreciation of being older in our modern world. Most magazines in the shops depict young, beautiful, glamorous people who conform to what advertising tells us is the perfect size. Of course, most of them are airbrushed by computers to look like that. I laugh at the Oscars ceremony, where a lot of the actresses dress in gold or beige with tanned skin and honey blonde hair. They all look the same, to my mind a bit like a female version of the gold statuette itself. I love to see the European actresses appear rounder, more voluptuous and with bold, colourful dresses. Something different, something original, something individual. There's a magazine ad I saw for bathroom fittings a while ago with a very beautiful naked grey-haired woman. She was stunning in her platinum beauty. The male version was so handsome too. I bet that ad caught lots of people's eye as it was so different. We need to realise that the so-called fountain of youth is how we live, look after ourselves and our attitude to life.

MY AUSTRALIAN EXPERIENCE

I was very fortunate to visit Uluru in Central Australia in 2012. This massive red rock in the outback desert is a major sacred site to the Anangu people, who are the Aboriginal custodians of the site. In a magically serendipitous way, I ended up with my husband, John, around a campfire under the full moon and stars with some friends and two Aboriginal elders, one of whom was the tribe's medicine man. Understandably these strong, gentle people are reticent to discuss their sacred ways in public as their history up until fairly recently has been very turbulent. That night, however, they did open up, sharing healing methods but in total confidence, which I completely respect so will not be writing about that. Both these men, brothers in their seventies, were known as 'elders' and referred to as 'uncle' by those younger than them as a mark of respect and an acknowledgement that they have life experience of value. Their ways of living were untouched until the 1780s when Europeans arrived and took over their lands. One of the brothers had been 'stolen' away from his family as a child as that was part of the European way of 'civilising' the indigenous people. After a very tough time he eventually returned to his family. Forgiveness is a big part of their medicine ways and it has helped him move on personally from that traumatic experience. Not all of his people can do that and as a race they are adrift in a modern world not of their making. I thought of our country's history of emigration and how many of our older generation living abroad, especially in the UK, are homeless or on the poverty line, afraid to return to a country they no longer recognise or feel part of.

A TELLING STORY

I once had a client who had a very interesting dilemma. Her loving, energetic and dynamic husband suddenly, overnight became an old man, complete with pipe and slippers, and was morphing into a couch potato. She couldn't get any explanation from him nor could she fathom why. He wasn't ill, was past retirement age, which had gone smoothly, and there was no trauma or unusual circumstances. Eventually we worked it out. He had reached an age where in his mind he was 'past it'. He had an image of his father and grandfather at that age, and so, he subconsciously copied them. He gave up living life, felt he had nothing to say and was out of touch.

The fact that he lived in a very different world to both his predecessors hadn't been factored into his equation. With patience and gentle persuasion, his wise wife brought this to his attention and coaxed him out of it. He was lucky to have such an astute woman in his life.

TIPS TO TRY

We need to be our own wise advisor and figure out how to be, look and behave as we age. Our parents may not have been the best examples. Remember they lived in a very different world. Even though we are feeling the effects of post-pandemic years and difficult economic situations, we are still infinitely better off than our predecessors. A generation ago it was commonplace to leave school at fourteen years of age and be compelled to bring in a wage straight away. In the above example of my client's husband, his father and grandfather were not particularly good models as he was fit, healthy and had more energy to do lots more living than they had. Take a little quiet time to assess if you are keeping up with life or slipping behind and losing touch. Don't panic if you feel you are; just figure out your next move carefully. Also ask for help from a family member or friend. It is worth the time and effort, and you will reap the benefits through increased self-esteem.

WORDS OF WISDOM

Name: Ināra Semeika.

Country of origin: Latvia.

Country of habitation: Latvia.

Age: Eighty.

Occupation: Mechanical drafter (mechanical engineer), wife, mother and grandmother.

1. What do you wish you had done or started earlier in your life?

I would plant trees of different varieties so I could see how they grow.

2. What are you delighted you did or started earlier in your life?

I'm happy that I always have lived an active lifestyle – I love walking and gardening, so I'm delighted that we always had a dog to walk so from spring until autumn time this would keep me going. I always walk to the shops and would take stairs instead of elevators so I am still fit and healthy.

RENT A GRANNY

Wouldn't it be fantastic to have such a wonderful thing as a professional granny or grandad? There are so many children who don't have grandparents around on a daily basis. They may not live nearby or may have passed away since many people are having children later in life. Then there are a lot of lonely older people with time on their hands. Imagine if we matched them up and all babysitters were older people like the character in the film *Mrs. Doubtfire*? Of course, they wouldn't have the same energy as younger babysitters but they would have fabulous stories, terrific games and time to listen. Grandparents have a big role to play in society.

Many people love their granny or grandad having experienced the unconditional love on offer. Perhaps grandparents have the freedom to give what they did not have the chance to as parents. I have met quite a few people that are absolutely mystified by the fact that their offspring have huge regard for their grandparents when they felt that they weren't particularly good as parents when they were children. As we age, we become more experienced and wiser with extra time to be there for young grandchildren in a way that we never could as busy parents. A colleague recognised that her mother, who caused her great grief in life growing up, has somehow morphed into an excellent granny. She's not sure how but has to grudgingly admit that her son adores her mum, his granny.

ROLE MODELS

Modern society loves youth and beauty but why can't we revere character and wisdom too? Who do we look to as role models on how to be in our old age? It might be our parents or grandparents or it could be a prominent member of society. Helen Mirren is one of my heroines. She is so sexy and confident in her seventies. Judi Dench is another, fabulous in her eighties. Closer to home, we have Mary Robinson and Mary McAleese. It is important to remember that we are the future ancestors. We are the role models for the next generation. So, let's dream big and invent wonderful ways to be older so that young people can look forward to the future with excitement rather than trepidation. I so enjoy reading the brochure of the Bealtaine Festival in Ireland every May. It is a terrific month-long celebration of creativity in old age by older people for older people. My mother loves it, and she and her friends regale me with their adventures each year. It is a brilliant way of promoting greater participation by older people, and is championed by Age & Opportunity, an organisation working to enable the best possible quality of life for us all as we age. It is a perfect illustration that there are heroes and heroines all around us who are wonderful role models, living life to the maximum.

Another initiative called Aosdána was set up by the Arts Council in 1981 to honour artists with outstanding contributions in Ireland. Over the years, there have been seven Saoi (wise ones) voted for by their peers in recognition of their sustained distinction, among them are Brian Friel, Seamus Heaney and Camille Souter. Most of them tend to be older, and I like to think of them as State-recognised artistic Irish elders.

WORDS OF WISDOM
Name: Dona Maria Apaza Machaca.
Country: The High Mountain Village of Quiqo, The Qero Nation, Peru, and recently Cusco, Peru.

Age: Eighty-four.

Occupation: *Alto Mesayoq*/Andean priestess healer, farmer of potatoes, corn, alpacas, sheep and cattle, wife, mother, grandmother and now great-grandmother.

1. What do you wish you had done or started earlier in your life?

Karen: This was quite extraordinary for me. Dona Maria had no concept of anything in her life that she had wanted to do and hadn't actually done. Through her friend, apprentice and translator Luis Alejo Mango, I reworded the question in several different ways but still no answer. Luis assured me that Maria did understand the question but she had lived her life as she wanted to. Of course, she did have the usual ups and downs in life including being struck by lightning three times – the sign of one ordained to be a healer. However, her natural beliefs and medicine ways gave her the tools to deal with these. She has buried two husbands and has reared her five children and introduced some of them to her healing skills. She is now in her eighties travelling across the planet to fulfil her destiny as she sees it – to teach her indigenous healing ways to the people of the North (the USA and Europe including Ireland) for balance of all the children of Mother Earth.

2. What are you delighted you did or started earlier in your life?

I wished to be a great healer for my family and community, so I learned to be free and have an open heart. I learned to connect to the light of the sun, moon and great stars, the mountains and their protector hills, Mother Earth, the mighty seas and the light of all the elements of our cosmos. I give my gratitude daily as I share their beauty. I am open to receiving the light of all that is [this is what Maria understands God to be] and I teach others how to share and teach this too. From my heart I walk in beauty every day. My wisdom to your readers is to live from an open heart, love, be free and connect to our Mother Earth's beauty every day.

Chapter Seven MENTAL ADJUSTMENT

STUCK IN A RUT

Have you ever met a fifty-two-year-old teenager? Or a seventy-year-old overprotective mother? In my work I frequently do. Let me explain. Sometimes we get stuck at certain important phases in our life. So, while we grow up physically, we don't mature mentally. If you were a mummy's boy or a daddy's girl, that was fine as a phase, but you do need to grow out of it and stop behaving in the same way when you become an adult. There are certain key stages of life that we all need to go through and if we miss out on them, our growth is stunted. Many Irish people who never leave home as a young adult don't know how to fend for themselves. Then if they do marry, they expect their partners to look after them in the same way their mother or father did. As a consequence, some women marry a man very like their father and instead of an adult relationship swap one protective man who looks after them for another. Often they can't take responsibility for their life path. There are a lot of Irish men who married a surrogate mother who irons their shirts and mollycoddles them in a mother–son type of relationship.

 TIPS TO TRY

Having an awareness of these types of patterns goes a long way to resolving them. We need to look long and hard at any patterns of behaviour that mimic childhood or teenage moods and replace them with healthier ones. A professional counsellor can help with this, and many wonderful counsellors can be found through the Irish Association of Counselling and Psychotherapy (www.iacp.ie). We need to move into and through old age in a healthy way mentally, forging ahead and learning from our inevitable mistakes.

MOVING ON

We can also become stuck and stop maturing after we experience a traumatic event. In that case we may need to revisit the experience alone or with help to gain insight, forgive, forget and move on. Otherwise, we could just become bitter and obstruct our natural growth. There are a lot of people on this planet carrying around virtual mountains of old hurts and grievances on their shoulders, which means they can't overcome that difficult situation. Therefore, they relive the old emotions time and time again, or repress them until they bubble out, which may be in the form of a physical illness. It takes maturity and courage to move on, yet many of us are never taught how to do it. There is a difference between revisiting and reliving any past experiences. The former is cathartic and the latter may be as traumatic as the first time it happened. More than likely the person who hurt you isn't thinking about you all these years later so why would you let them continue to upset you? I think my hero Nelson Mandela is a terrific example for this. After twenty-seven years in prison, many in solitary confinement, he forgave his captors. He often said that even locked up in his tiny cell he was freer than the men who guarded him. He knew that he had a choice to let them affect him or to keep his soul free.

TIPS TO TRY
One way of doing this is to use the technique of putting ourselves in the other person's shoes and trying to envisage

what they could have been experiencing to do what they did. We can gain valuable insight when looking at the problem from the other point of view. In the process of maturing, we reach a stage where we need to stop blaming others and take responsibility for our part. This is a difficult thing to do and may take time. Forgiveness is an amazing virtue to have and if we can reach that stage, then we are truly free of the constraints of the problem for good. We need to be strong and brave to do this, even if it means saying the words privately through gritted teeth as opposed to actually facing the person who hurt us. We can then safely rewire our old ways of thinking and stop reliving the bad experiences time and time again. People get stuck with all sorts of challenges. This technique helps hugely with relationship stagnation, family rows, sibling rivalry, work-related problems and arguments with friends.

Sometimes an old hurt can seem unsurmountable but when teased out is quite simple to rationalise and come to terms with. I often equate it with seeing a child run in from play covered in blood. A terrifying sight. Yet when cleaned up it may really only be a scratch. In other words, it looks much worse than it actually is. Other times what seems like a trivial hurt might reveal a much deeper wound that will fester if not attended to.

SURVIVAL MECHANISMS

Perhaps at a difficult time in your life you had to adopt an instinctual survival mechanism to get by. This may have saved your life or at least your sanity, but what happens when the situation passes and you are still in survival mode? It may now transpire that the lifesaver is now part of the problem. It could be that you were in a relationship that was abusive. This sounds like a very serious scenario and it is. 'Abuse' is a strong word and we may associate it with physical or sexual harm. Yet how many of us have been in relationships where the abuse was verbal or even emotional, where you were constantly put down or not rated? This, while not life threatening, can hugely affect our personal worth and self-esteem. Let's imagine that because of this you began to close your heart so that you couldn't be hurt anymore. I'd say it was very effective at the time and helped you remove yourself from the relationship or indeed manage to live with it. The important question is: did you ditch the survival mechanism when the situation was over? Maybe not and that can have serious repercussions as you try to move into a new and healthy relationship.

You might need to take a good, hard look at any situation where you went into survival mode to make sure that you have safely come out of it when the danger has passed. If you have changed enough to recognise the dynamic, then the chances are that you will not attract the same sort of partner again.

CHEEKY ANGEL/CHEEKY DIVIL

Are you aware of your inner dialogue, which can be positive or negative? Most people listen to the little 'cheeky divil' voice that reminds us of our mistakes and all the things we do wrong. What they may not realise is that this negative inner critic will always speak first to alert us to anything that we need to change so we don't repeat our mistakes. Once we acknowledge this *then* we can readily listen to the 'cheeky angel' voice that is our positive inner coach and urges us on to bigger and better things. If we just listened to the positive, then we'd constantly repeat errors and if we just listened to the negative, then we'd probably never take any risks or try anything new. We need to acknowledge both inner voices with the knowledge that it's negative first then positive and make sure we move from one to the other.

TIPS TO TRY
Did you ever write down your inner thoughts? This is a very interesting exercise and can tell us a lot about our mental

health. Bring a notebook with you for a day and jot down your thoughts every so often. Monitor them with a rating scale from one to ten, where one is a very negative thought and ten is a very positive thought. See how you do and if the scale tips in the direction of the positive then all is well. If you are constantly thinking negative thoughts, then it is time to soul-search why before doing something about it to bring balance into your way of thinking.

FORGETFULNESS

Have you reached the stage yet where your memory isn't as good as it used to be? For example, walking upstairs and then forgetting why you went up in the first place. Did you ever have a chat with an older relative who halfway through a conversation stops, trying to remember names and details that don't exactly enhance the story? In the effort to remember they become frustrated and you probably get bored.

In my daily meditation I ream off a list of special items – a mixture of people who inspire me and natural beauties that I love. It's a way to start my day with a strong positive intent, asking for guidance and support. Of course, I'm also exercising my mind by remembering the sacred list. This private practice has a huge spiritual and mental benefit for me. I bet that was one of the reasons behind saying long prayers in the various different religions and why the ancient Irish storytellers, the Bards, learnt their tales off by heart.

 TIPS TO TRY

When you reach that stage in life where your memory is not what it used to be, simply decide to tell the story and if you forget a detail, then just leave it out. Nobody will mind if the story is about a man you knew versus giving them his exact name. It is still the same story. Also, while we are on the subject of memory why not have a pair of glasses in every room so there is no need to search around for them?

The alternative is to keep them on your head or buy a fancy chain and hang them around your neck for easy access. We all know about looking after our physical health but our mental health is just as important. Remember when we used to exercise our brains by reeling off phone numbers or totting up our grocery bill? A great way to keep our mental capacity in fine fettle is to do crosswords, play sudoku, bridge or bingo. The latter two are terrific as they provide a social element as well.

Keep your mind stimulated by joining your local library, if you haven't already. As well as stocking information on a host of local events and classes, the range of books available is impressive. If there's one you can't find, they will order it and have it ready in less than a week. There's nothing quite like immersing yourself in a good book to exercise your mind and broaden your horizons.

THE CRITICAL EYE

I have come across this concept personally and with clients. It can be a consequence of middle to old age because of habits of a lifetime. Basically, some of us require a keen eye for detail in our careers or as busy parents. For example, I can walk into any room and in sixty seconds appraise it for health and safety and a pleasing atmosphere. In all the years I worked as a therapist it was important to make sure my classes and clients were safe and in a nice environment.

The problems started when I began to bring my critical eye home. I could easily criticise my husband, my family and my home for what it wasn't, rather than love it and them for what it was. Thankfully I nipped it in the bud relatively early as I am a trained psychotherapist and so saw the unhelpful pattern. If I didn't, however, and had four children, a full-time job and a partner who reacted badly to my criticism, then the situation may not have been very conducive to a happy home.

TIPS TO TRY

Do you have a critical eye too? If so, where and when does it manifest? Are you always looking for what's wrong rather than what is right in your world? Awareness alone is an important key to changing this negative habit. Catch yourself about to fall into the trap and then distract yourself. Typically, easy ways to do this are to phone a friend, go outside for a breath of fresh air, sing your favourite song or take ten deep breaths. Finally start some positive self-talk along the lines of: 'The room the children are playing in is fine. They are having fun and we can clean up before bedtime'; or 'My husband just made a special dinner and I'm going to enjoy it before I clean up the mess in the kitchen. His forte is cooking and mine is cleaning so that's only fair.'

WORDS OF WISDOM

Name: Abi Moran.

Country of origin: England.

Country of habitation: Ireland.

Age: Seventy-four.

Occupation: Mother, wife, retired medical secretary.

1. What do you wish you had done or started earlier in your life?

My mother passed away in 1998. I wish that I had listened more to her wisdom and her precise language, acquired more of her knowledge and style, learnt more about our family history and appreciated her accomplishments and love.

2. What are you delighted you did or started earlier in your life?

I am glad I married my husband, lived in Ireland and brought up my beautiful sons. I learnt that nothing is as good as it seems and nothing is as bad as it seems.

CHAOTIC WAYS

Do you ever, due to stress or depression, become messy and untidy, not really caring how your home looks as you haven't the energy to maintain it? I have a classic personal sign when I am starting to let things slide. I don't wash my hair for a few days and slob around in my pyjamas each evening instead of going out for a walk. Once I observe this, I sit and figure out what is the source of the issue. I might seek help from my husband or a close family member. Frequently clients come to my clinic having let a similar situation develop over years to the detriment of their relationships. Sometimes I hear about one partner with a critical eye and the other with chaotic ways – a recipe for disaster!

All we have to do is look to nature to see that order and routine are important in life. The seasons teach us how to live well. Spring brings in the new birth of life after the death of winter. Summer flowers come to fruition in autumn. There is a constant cycle of natural birth, death and rebirth.

 TIPS TO TRY

Make sure to let old things go to make room for the new. There is nothing inherently wrong with being a bit messy. Try to take notice of when your pattern of living changes and ask yourself if that is a good thing. If not, then you need to do something about it. As humans we are creatures of habit whether we like to admit it or not. In your day, do you usually eat three meals, work for eight hours, relax or play for four to six, and sleep for approximately eight hours? A good routine will keep you on track, bringing order and security.

PARENTING OUR PARENTS

A true sign of ageing is when we realise it is time to parent our own parents. Just as they looked after us when we were babies and children, life comes full circle and we now may be the ones to look after them. At some stage we wanted our parents to care for us as best they could and if they didn't do a good enough job then we may be critical of them. Yet when they become older and the tables are turned, we may find out that it's not so easy. There can be all sorts of difficult sibling rivalry and heartache in this type of scenario. More often than not the single daughter is the one who ends up looking after aged parents because other siblings are busy with their children. They can forget that the single sister has a life too, it just may not involve a partner or children. Older, ill mothers may want their daughters to tend to them, which can alienate sons or let them off the hook. Adult children who live abroad are in another bind, missing out on valuable special time at the end of their parent's life or receiving a major guilt trip from their brothers and sisters who are doing the lion's share of the caring at home.

The ideal scenario is a family meeting where feelings are discussed openly and honestly. Those away from home might contribute financially or arrange holidays to give the ones at home a break. I also highly recommend encouraging the older or ill parents to sort out their affairs early as so many families are torn apart by either a lack of a will or an unexplained one.

I know a family where two brothers didn't talk for years over the fact that it seemed the father had favoured one over the other in his will. Eventually an old aunt made a chance comment that the reason for this was that the mother had done the same in reverse years earlier, and the father wanted to redress the balance as he loved both equally. However, because the mother left a specific item that only one brother wanted, nobody noticed. The cold facts of the father's written will didn't explain his emotional reasons.

FINANCES
As we age there may be a huge mental adjustment to loss of earnings and having to live off a pension or reduced income. It is hard to see into the future and predict what will happen. I am quite sceptical about pension schemes and

relying on them totally. The way our population is growing at the moment there will be a reduced workforce supporting a majority of older people. I have a funny feeling that the money we pay in today will not give us the return we think it might in the future. I'm planning to do some sort of work in the holistic area for my health and self-esteem as long as I can. What helps is that I don't work in a job where I am living to retire and 'get out' at some stage.

In an ideal world we will have our mortgage paid off and no loans after our children are educated. Our lifestyle will be simpler and we will have our homes furnished. It is well worth doing a quick tot up now in your middle years to see if you are on target for that sort of peace of mind in the future.

COMPLEXES

As we age it is easy to end up with a chip on our shoulder. We have to face who we are and how we are living. We may not like how our life has turned out so far or feel as though we haven't fulfilled our potential. If so, then we need to stop whining, shake ourselves off and just do it, or at least a version of it. I always admired the movers and shakers in our society until recently it dawned on me with a shock that I'm of the age that either I become one or I miss out and watch from the sidelines. Of course, I might be happy to do so, depending on what I feel is my life's destiny. It took me until my thirties to find out where I fit in. Holistic health resonates deeply within me. Although I fought it for years, I came to know that I have a gift for teaching the workshops I facilitate with my husband, John, working one to one with clients and in the way I write. Not a learn-off-by-heart type of teaching, but by example and by creating discussions in which others come to their own insights. I am a fairly ordinary woman, who makes mistakes and is very human, but who has an open heart and loves to learn and intends to do so until the day I die.

WORDS OF WISDOM

Name: David Patrick Bernard FitzPatrick Norris.

Country of origin: Africa.

Country of habitation: Ireland.

Age: Seventy-seven.

Occupation: Public representative.

1. What do you wish you had done or started earlier in your life?

I wish I had taken seriously physical exercise. I do believe in the old Roman tag *Mens sana in corpore sano*. In late middle age I went to the gym and found it a wonderful and friendly environment, but sadly that gym has closed. The relationship, for example, between good breathing and good mental health is one to which I continually return.

2. What are you delighted you did or started earlier in your life?

I am delighted that I play the piano and learnt to appreciate music; that I developed the habit of reading and of travelling. I shall continue to travel as long as I can and when that stops, I shall continue to travel mentally through reading.

Chapter Eight   WISDOM

WHAT IS IT?
Some would say wisdom is the knowledge we glean from
books. Many would say it is a culmination of our experience.
I agree with the latter but think it is more than just that. It
is also the intuitive insights we gain on life's journey. It is
not enough to have had life experiences and then remember
them. That is easy enough to do. Wisdom is about gaining
insight from them and then moving on. Not everyone will be
able to do that.

A LIFE LESSON
I remember a situation from childhood. I was stacking
shopping in a cupboard as a new part of my household jobs.
Since I was bored, I was doing it badly. I wanted to be outside
playing with my friends. My dad, frustrated by my slow
efforts, gave out to me, urging me to do it again properly. I
felt angry, and was sulky and ashamed. Then my wonderful
grand-aunt Lily appeared and she sat down beside me. I asked
her what she wanted and she replied, 'Oh, just to be with you.'
I continued in silence. Eventually she asked what I was doing.
I told her, 'I have to stack these packets on the shelf and there
isn't enough room so they keep falling off.' She asked me if
this was a new task that nobody had ever done before. Of
course, it wasn't. My mother did it every week. The penny
dropped. There was a way to do this; I just didn't know how.

Now Lily had piqued my curiosity, set me a personal challenge turning the task into a game. I tried to picture how best to do it, having watched my mother a million times, and eventually remembered that she turned the items on their side so she could see each label clearly, leaving enough room for every one of them. With a growing sense of excitement, I changed the way I had been working and successfully began to stock the shelves neatly. All the while my old grand-aunt sat with me quietly nodding her head and smiling her encouragement. This was her wisdom at work. My dad didn't have the time to instruct me. He and my mother were very busy and probably stressed with the six of us milling about. Lily had the time and the insight. More than likely the same thing had happened to her when she was a girl. I actually like packing shelves to this day as I recognised the learning experience and the sense of wisdom I picked up. Someday perhaps the opportunity will arise and I can also pass this onto my younger nieces and nephews.

HOW TO HAVE A WISE DAY

Life will have its highs and lows. While we all love and relish the highs – a beautiful sunset, a successful outcome with a client, a moving moment with a loved one – we probably won't learn anything much from these very special encounters. However, when we have a low – a challenge, a depressing day or frustration at work – we have an opportunity to figure out how to overcome it while learning something valuable.

When we experience a big high, we need to realise that we cannot hold onto them but learn to know that they will pass, trusting that there will be more in time. After the big high, there will inevitably be a big low soon enough. The post-holiday blues are a good example. Again, we can't avoid them but must ride the storm, trusting that there will be another high followed also by another low. It is important to note that on a low, we might be susceptible to stagnation. There may be a temptation to become bitter and wallow for weeks on end while giving our power away and blaming someone or something else. Have you done this in the past and now recognise that it didn't get you anywhere?

TIPS TO TRY
You might consider having a wise day. To do this, go through your normal day as usual but with an awareness of the wise things you are doing or saying (or not saying as the case may be). You might recognise that doing daily Pilates exercises and meditation in the morning is wise because if you leave it until later, you might not be able to find the time. You might see that commenting to your partner on what they forgot to do when they are hungry or tired is not the wisest move, but later when rested and fed you can both chat about what needs to be done together. Perhaps choose something special to do each evening as an incentive to power you through the day so that if you are flagging you have a treat to look forward to. The wisest thing might be to keep your treats to the non-chocolate variety during the week. All bets are off at the weekend and Saturday night might be a mini chocolate fest, 70 per cent, of course!

AWARENESS OF WISDOM
Once you become attuned to the presence of true wisdom in your life then every day becomes a fabulous arena for spotting it at work in the world. Many years ago, I had tickets for the aftershow party of major music awards in Dublin. My friend and I decided to watch them on TV first so we would know who won when we arrived later on. I went down to the corner shop to get some popcorn and nachos, and the old man behind the counter asked me if I was having a party. I replied, 'Ah, no, the big awards are on but I only have an invite to the party afterwards.' He looked at me intently and said, 'Wherever you're at is where it's at.' I was bowled over. Such words of wisdom! He was so right. How many times

have I been at a so-called amazing event that was just alright when often the most spectacular things happen in the most mundane of circumstances? Of course, I don't know if he was even aware of the words of wisdom he was passing on but they were so profound for me. I had a new appreciation for the specialness of spending time with my girlfriend, hanging out at home, having a laugh watching the show on television. Indeed, the big aftershow party was great fun and we rubbed shoulders with some of the greats of the music industry but it was even more fun because of our connection, our sharing of the experience at home first.

OLD WAYS, NEW TWIST
I studied holistic therapies for many years, including reflexology, reiki, aromatherapy massage and shamanism. All of these are ancient ways of healing practised in a modern world. Sometimes people are surprised at my use of the word 'holistic' rather than 'alternative' to refer to this type of work. I feel we need to work like Hippocrates, the ancient Greek father of medicine who combined nutritionists, massage therapists, yoga or t'ai-chi-like exercise instructors with the equivalent of nurses, counsellors, energy therapists, spiritual advisors, doctors and surgeons in his clinic. All have a place in our healthcare as far as I am concerned. To me today's modern medical centres are bringing back this ancient concept in a modern capacity. I regularly receive referrals from local doctors for counselling psychotherapy work and indeed I have referred clients back to their own doctor. One very wise GP gave his older, recently widowed patient a prescription to rescue a dog from the pound. She was bemused and reluctantly decided to give it a go. He knew that she missed her beloved husband, was lonely and had no reason to go outside for fresh air, exercise and social contact. That little bundle of four-legged joy was her saviour, as was she to Rover, who might have been put down if no one had come to his rescue. The doctor's inspired advice changed two lives for the better.

WORDS OF WISDOM

Name: Eimear Burke.

Country of origin: Ireland.

Country of habitation: Ireland.

Age: Sixty-two.

Occupation: Psychologist, healer.

1. What do you wish you had done or started earlier in your life?

I wish I had trusted my own inner knowing and wisdom sooner, and broken through restrictive cultural norms which would have allowed me to be true to myself.

2. What are you delighted you did or started earlier in your life?

I lived overseas in different places in my twenties. This broadened my world view and helped me to take a path into becoming a healer and has given me an appreciation of nature and my relationship to it. It has given me a deeper connection with my own indigenous landscape. This allows me to live a more authentic life.

A WISE OWL

I am fascinated by owls. I love their sleek shape, their eerie call and their piecing glare as though they are looking into my very soul. Most of the time I see their image in photographs and on television programmes. To my delight I visited a bird of prey rescue sanctuary in Sligo where these magnificent creatures are nursed back to health when they are injured in the wild, along with eagles, hawks and other similar wild birds. For the first time I had an opportunity to see owls at close quarters. They are truly amazing to behold. I watched in rapt awe as they swooped through the air a few feet above me in a dance of feathered movement. However, I was a bit perturbed by the sight of the leg ring that, as I thought, tied them to their perch. When I asked why, I learnt an astonishing fact.* Owls

* In the sanctuary the birds of prey are kept safe on their perch/home especially the younger ones. When they are getting used to crowds, they can get flustered and fly off if they are not tied to their perch. It's a bit like toddlers on safety reins.

spend most of their time sitting in their nest or tree doing nothing. They only move to catch food for themselves or their young, to mate, to exercise a few times a day and if there is danger. They conserve their energy until they need to move, not needlessly spending it on unnecessary flight. Hence the wisdom they are often associated with. This made complete sense to me especially as I age. A swallow is a swallow and by its very nature it moves constantly, but an owl is a very different creature. It knows how to be an owl and doesn't try to be anything else.

TIPS TO TRY

Why would we expect to run around with the energy of a teenager or the busyness of youth when we are older? We need to respect and conserve our energy for when we need it. A wise woman in her sixties once said that she has the same energy as she had in her forties except only for 60 per cent of the time. What a beautiful observation. The next time you lie on in the morning, take a siesta or have quiet time in the evening, don't feel guilty but know that you are conserving your energy wisely like our feathered owl friends.

THE WISDOM OF HOLIDAYS

You might be wondering where the wisdom element is in taking a holiday. Surely it is a time of rest, a treat and that's all. In my workshops, classes and clinic I have seen at close quarters the effects of *not* taking a holiday and it isn't pretty. Lethargy, mild depression and flatness are only a few of the symptoms I've observed. Indeed, I can't stress enough the importance of taking time out to unwind, relax and change your routine. Our bodies and minds valiantly trudge along, doing their very best for us on a daily basis and every so often it really pays to stop, take a break and do nothing. Some people reason that with their economic situation it is better not to pay for expensive holidays and to keep working.

Some literally can't find the time to take a break. This is false wisdom as instead we begin to work at a slower pace and are not as effective as we would be if we had taken the holiday in the first place. Think back to the rejuvenation after some time away – the feelings of renewal and increased sense of worth, not to mention seeing the world from a different perspective.

TIPS TO TRY
When was the last time you took a holiday? Are you due to go on one soon? If money is tight, can you be creative and shop around for inexpensive special deals or go to a friend's place instead of a hotel? A weekend break will give you a change of scenery and a shot of vigour. A week-long break will slow the rhythm of your regular routine but a two-week holiday will change the pace of your body systems and gift you a feeling of renewal. A good tip is to tell your loved ones that you don't intend to send postcards (unless you really want to) as it can take up a lot of time and energy to find, write and post them. You might even be home before they arrive. As regards holiday presents, do you really need to spend money and time on them? I tend to buy some small inexpensive local food delicacy as a thought rather than clogging up my relative's shelves with souvenirs they don't need or want. When you visit a new country, consider purchasing one decent souvenir item for yourself that reflects the culture or traditions there, rather than loading down your luggage with many smaller knick-knacks that will only gather dust at home.

WORDS OF WISDOM
Name: Adna (Asna) Warner (née Berkivitz).
Country of origin: England.
Country of habitation: Leeds, England.
Age: Ninety-two.
Occupation: Hairdresser, beautician, wife, mother of four, Jewish.

1. What do you wish you had done or started earlier in your life?

I wish I'd married an army officer and not the one my Mum made me marry. I wish I had learnt to drive and gone abroad to see more of the world.

2. What are you delighted you did or started earlier in your life?

I am proud of my fifteen grandchildren and that everyone in the family is unified. I always kept £200 in a secret drawer that my husband never knew about in case anything happened and I needed it. Each birthday, when everyone was out, I'd put on disco music, dance like a maniac, look in the mirror and feel only fifteen!

Chapter Nine   NEW WAYS OF BEING

REINVENTING YOURSELF
I have been fascinated by the concept of reinventing yourself
at certain times of life. I did it very successfully twice. The first
time I emigrated to London in the late 1980s. I presented
myself to my English friends and colleagues as 'the new me'.
I became more self-assured and confident than I had been at
home. It was much easier to do the reinvention thing when I
moved into a situation where I could 'act as if' and become
the 'me' that I knew I could be without my family wondering
what I was at. It was important to know that I was still 'me'
but changing in a joyous quantum leap rather than the
usual slower step by step. The next time I did it, I changed
career. I had been in the very busy world of marketing and
public relations, which ranged from science subjects to the
arts, fashion and events. In the meantime, I was studying
a plethora of holistic subjects part-time. I dropped from a
five-day back to a four-day and finally a three-and-a-half-
day week, before I took the plunge and became a full-
time holistic therapist. When I started working in a local
leisure centre, I changed my wardrobe overnight from suits
with high heels to stretchy yoga gear and funky runners.
Naturally, nobody in the new job thought that was odd as
they expected a yoga teacher and relaxation therapist to
dress like that. Only I knew the huge change that had taken
place. People that I hadn't seen in years hardly recognised

me. I grew into this phase from an environment that accepted readily my new way of being.

TIPS TO TRY
Retirement is a great time to do this since you may no longer have to wear a suit or a certain look now that you are in a different environment all day. You will be free to develop a fresh routine based around your needs. For example, when you arrive for the first time at the local bowling, bridge or active retirement club, reinvent yourself. Leave behind the old stressed, busy-every-minute you and introduce them to the laid-back, chilled-out you. It will certainly feel strange at first and if you have any acting skills, these will help. Soon you will shake off every vestige of the old traits you have actively chosen to leave behind and embrace the ones you have yearned for. Of course, you can use the same principle when you change jobs. This could include moving from the role of a busy parent to a retiree.

REGRET

This is a huge area that deserves some serious contemplation. I recently met three women and two men in their late forties who have major regrets in life. Yet they are still young and have a lot of opportunity to turn their life around – if they really want to. This is the crux of the matter. Some of us are stuck and can only voice the regrets while not being able to figure out what to do next. It might be a case of the devil you know, rather than the devil you don't, as the old saying goes. In other words, you are comfortable in your stuckness, possibly receiving a lot of attention because of it, which creates a loop that is hard to break free of.

MISSING SOCIAL CUES

I know one woman who is obsessed with what people think of her as she feels she isn't liked. When she talks, incessantly, she doesn't make eye contact, misses everyone's reaction to what she is saying and rarely listens. The consequence? People politely avoid her company and her self-fulfilling prophecy occurs again and again and again. At some level she knows something isn't right and that is why she is conscious of what people think of her; however, because she doesn't listen or watch the reaction to what she is saying, she has no way of knowing what is going wrong. She wonders why she has no close friends or a partner. She is an intelligent, professional woman with a good job but, somehow, she just missed a few classic social habits and is now floundering. It is a tough situation to be in. You might be wondering could family and friends step in and take her aside. If they did, would she listen to them or blame them for her woes? Many of us look down or up or anywhere but at the person we are talking to. How can we then know if we are boring or entrancing them? Do you look directly at the people you are talking and listening to?

TIPS TO TRY

We regularly need to take a long, hard look at ourselves and see if we are the architects of our own downfalls. How often have you heard someone bemoan that 'nobody understands me' or 'they all pick on me' or 'I never get the breaks I deserve'? Maybe it's time to point the finger backwards and take the blame ourselves. It is so easy to wallow in self-pity and think that everyone else has a magic life that unfolds amazingly well whereas ours is in chaos. We need to take responsibility for our *own* life. Nobody has a totally charmed existence. That is a fallacy. Everyone has challenges, just some people know how to deal with life's ups and downs better than others.

I'll give you a small example. I noticed that when a beloved sister came to visit, because I knew her really well, I would open the door with a quick hello and say, 'I'm just finishing what I am doing on the computer, so put the kettle on. I'll be there in a minute.' Of course, it was never a minute and, without realising it, I was being blatantly rude to someone very special to me. How long before she stopped calling over or thought that she wasn't important to me? Something so simple could have major effects on someone's self-esteem. Imagine my adult sister was my young teenage niece? See the possible consequences?

Once a year, it's a great idea to take stock of who you are and where you are going in life. A brilliant time to do this is on holiday as you have time to yourself out of your normal routine. Start by assessing your year. Are you pleased with how it has gone so far? Are there any areas that are not going very well? Why? What about your relationships? Again, is all well or not? Make a note if anything needs to be looked at and brainstorm what to do about it. Finally, begin to think about your future from work and family to hobbies and dreams. Are you meandering along in life or winging it half the time? It's a good idea to put in place a decent five-year plan. You can always change or add to it later.

WORDS OF WISDOM
Name: Eleanor Harty.
Country of origin: Co. Dublin, Ireland.
Country of habitation: Co. Carlow, Ireland.
Age: Seventy-eight.
Occupation: Secretary, mother of five, market researcher, complementary therapist (reiki, integrated energy therapy, shamanism, crystals, mysticism).
1. What do you wish you had done or started earlier in your life?
I had to put my 'true life' (my mind, body, spiritual life) on hold while being a wife and a mother until I was in my sixties. It was only then I discovered my soul.
2. What are you delighted you did or started earlier in your life?
I felt old at forty so I did something about it – I did courses in proofreading and editing that let me know my brain was

still active. I also returned to my hobby of theatre-going and a regular day out in Dublin, which I've continued since then.

GREY NOMADS

I came across this term, 'grey nomads', for the first time in Australia. It describes retired couples that buy camper vans and travel all over the country for months and sometimes years. They may be visiting their children and relations who live in different parts of Australia or sightseeing places that they couldn't travel to earlier in life due to family or work commitments. What an amazing concept. We met some of them at Uluru and Kata Tjuta and they formed a sort of informal club where they chat at the picnic tables and swap stories, routes and even food. Of course, we have a European version too. I'm sure many of you have seen German or French older couples in their camper vans here in Ireland. I haven't seen the Irish equivalent yet but they must be out there somewhere. It may sound like a fantastic new idea but, in fact, whether the grey nomads know it or not, they are following a time-old tradition of the elders of old. At a certain age when the children were reared and the apprentices were trained to take over, an older couple would assess their lives. Did they want to be together? If no, then they would split amicably and divide their property and goods. If yes, then they would pare down their worldly possessions and go travelling nomadic style, sharing their wisdom with other tribes, preparing the younger ones at key life stages. Many indigenous tribes the world over had their version of this phenomenon.

THE LINEAGE TEST

Here is a very interesting technique to really find out who you are, where you have come from and what you may evolve into. It is based on the classic genogram, which is a pictorial version of someone's family tree, showing their relationships and hereditary patterns, indicating traits of behaviour and psychological factors. Invented by Murray Bowen in the 1970s and developed by Monica McGoldrick and Randy Gerson, genograms are now widely used by counsellors, psychotherapists, doctors, psychologists and educators to explain family dynamics to their clients. My adaptation looks at what you know about your recent ancestors and reveals any patterns that you may choose to enhance or change.

1. Take a piece of paper, write down all you know about the parents of your mother (or whoever held the mothering role for you); their name, all the details you know about their family of origin, such as were they the eldest, youngest, and so on.
2. Now start adding in what they were like. Use stories you have heard if you never met them. What was their upbringing like? Did they live in the country or a town? Were they well-to-do or struggling moneywise? When and how did they meet their husband or wife? How many children did they have? What type of lifestyle did they have? Were they happy or depressed? Did their love last? Did either of them drink too much or get depressed? What was happening in the environment they lived in? Was it during difficult times such as war or recession? Did any of these events affect them directly? If you were to give them a descriptive label, what would it be? For example, I hardly knew my granny but everyone said she was gentle and shy but kind.
3. Now do the same for the parents of your father (or whoever held the fathering role for you).
4. Finally, take each of your parents and answer the same questions for them so that you have a list for each of your grandparents on both sides and your parents themselves.
5. You are looking for patterns to help you understand their influences in your life and your current behaviours. The idea is not to blame them – they probably did their best in the circumstances they were

in – but to learn from their mistakes. For example, you might note that there is a pattern of artistic ways in your maternal line or that your father's people were very connected with nature. Equally, there could be a pattern of addictions or anger or gentleness.

6. Now make a new list. What were the best traits you inherited from them? This could be 'I have a great ability to make things happen and I get this from my grandfather' or 'I have a good work ethic from my granny and mother' or 'I love to knit and crochet and this comes from both my grandmothers'.

7. What were their not-so-good traits? This could be a dawning that your fiery temper comes from your father and your cyclical stagnation is directly from his mother.

8. With all this information, assess what you need to let go of? Perhaps you need to work on your temper and harness it so that you are assertive rather than out of control. What do you want to nurture and enhance as a gift from your family lineage? You might really want to garden like your grandmother or golf like your father.

We all make mistakes but we have a choice whether to perpetuate the same ones as our ancestors or to gain insight and progress. This technique can really bring home whether we are stuck in an old family blame game. You know the 'if so and so hadn't left their will to blah-blah then our family would be rich and I would have gone to a different school' type of thing. Let's be blunt here: it happened and you can't change it. As the young ones say, 'Build a bridge and get over it!' An unwise ancestor may have made a stupid mistake but do you have to perpetuate it over and over again? I'm not suggesting denying and burying our heads in the sand like an ostrich. Why not sit down and have a serious think about any patterns that may need to be changed. It will be the best thing you have ever done – it will set you free.

MAKING YOUR LIFE MATTER

This sounds a bit grandiose but let me explain. I was at a funeral recently to support someone who was distantly related to the decreased single man in his late forties. I was struck by the amount of men on their own at the burial. At the lunch afterwards, nobody told any anecdotes or funny stories about the man who had passed away, or spoke of his achievements and accomplishments. You see, nobody really knew him. He was a solitary chap who had lived with his mother and when she passed away, he stayed in the family home on his own. He lost his job due to ill health and started to go down to the pub every night. Most of the men at his funeral were his drinking buddies. I thought about how I would like my funeral to be. I hope that, although my loved ones will be sad at my physical loss, they will mostly be happy that I will be peaceful and content wherever I am. I would love friends and family to laugh about my idiosyncratic ways, telling stories of what I had done over my lifetime; how in some small way my life had helped or encouraged others. I would like the person who does my service to have known me. I felt sad at the passing of this middle-aged man who seemed not to have really lived his life to the full. He hadn't moved away from home or travelled, had a big relationship or connected to a wide variety of people. This man was by no means unique. There were and are thousands like him out there. Yet, by his passing he had a profound effect on me and how I will live the rest of my life. I'm guessing that others there were also encouraged to grab life by the lapels and live it for all it is worth.

THE GOOD ROOM

Did you have a 'good room' at home growing up? You know what I mean – a room that was probably only used when visitors came or at Christmas and on special occasions. Usually it housed the crystal glasses, fancy crockery and dining table. Do you have good clothes that you only wear now and again? Your Sunday best, so to speak? One day it dawned on me that *now* is the time to live fully so why was I waiting for a few sporadic events in the future to use my precious things? To my husband's amazement and relief, I took our fancy glasses and crockery out and we use them every day now. It felt so good to be surrounded by beautiful things that we actually used all the time. If something broke, so what? Then we buy a new one to replace it. No big deal.

TIPS TO TRY
Have a look around your home and see if you have any good things stashed away that are used infrequently. Can you consider bringing them out to be loved daily while boosting your self-esteem? Be the special guest in your own home. Wear your good clothes weekly and enjoy parading around feeling great and looking terrific. If, however, these clothes no longer fit you or you find items that you are not using enough, give them to a local recycling shop so someone else can enjoy them every day.

WORDS OF WISDOM
Name: Trista Hendren.
Country of origin: Portland, Oregon, USA.
Country of habitation: Bergen, Norway.
Age: Forty-seven.
Occupation: Writer, publisher.
1. What do you wish you had done or started earlier in your life?
Revelling in taking care of myself – and in delighting myself. For most of my life, everyone else came first. I wish I had saved more of that time for myself. In retrospect, not everyone deserved so much of me. I also wish I had been able to travel earlier in life and tried to provide opportunities for my children to do so. My first international trip – to Lebanon – opened my eyes to the world, which up until that point had been very small. It completely changed my life and broadened my perspective.

2. What are you delighted you did or started earlier in your life?

Eating well. My family of origin did not give me a good example of how to take care of myself overall. My first husband taught me a lot about eating wonderfully nutritious foods and got me into juicing and exercise. I imagine my health would be quite different today had I not changed that in my early twenties. I am also glad I left the Church my first year in college because it contributed to my low sense of worth throughout my childhood. I am grateful that I found feminism and Goddess spirituality soon after and was able to reframe my view of myself as a woman.

Chapter Ten   HOLISTIC VIEWPOINT

ALL ASPECTS OF LIFE
In earlier chapters I mentioned the physical aspects and the
mental adjustment of ageing; however, there are many other
very important parts of our whole make-up. There's our
creativity, our sexuality, our personal growth, our spirituality,
not to mention our sense of humour. We are the sum of all
these parts. At times, though, we can pigeonhole ourselves
into who we were or who we think we have become.

I'll give you an example. Imagine you have been a bank
manager all your life. Originally it was a financial post
awarded to someone who had moved up the ranks within
the banking system. In the 1980s there was a big shift to
marketing bank services and the emphasis moved to a more
sales or public relations type of role. With the crisis within
the financial sector from 2008, a firefighting aspect became
vital. That means that you might have started your banking
career with a fairly serious demeanour and with a number-
crunching capacity. Then you probably had to morph into a
cheery people person, thinking outside the box, leading the
banking team into previously uncharted marketing waters.
Finally, in the latter years, I'm guessing that a cool, calm
exterior must have been vital in a country faced with all those
financial challenges.

If you are now retired, who are you? Which of the roles
you played during your career really sums up the essence

of who you are now? Naturally, all of the parts are relevant but perhaps some more than others. There is a film from the nineties called *Runaway Bride*. Julia Roberts plays a character who has been engaged many times but never makes it down the aisle. In each relationship, she started to act like the man she was engaged to because she thought, subconsciously, that is what he would like her to be. She did this six times! Eventually she realised that to be fully alive she had to be her true self and she needed to find out who that was before she could finally fall in love with her life partner.

SEXY AT SEVENTY

How come nobody talks about the sexual part of love when we are older? Maybe it's because generally we shied away from thinking about our parents having sex, never mind our grandparents, or perhaps it is because by the time we get older our relationships are falling apart so lovemaking is not a feature of life anymore? From what I have heard (and it's not everyone who will talk about this), it's all about quality rather than quantity. It is a slow, languid time of caressing, with a build up to a glorious climax, rather than the excitement of a quick and passionate romp. Not to say that there is no passion or excitement when you are older or indeed slow languidness when you are younger. I am generalising here to explain the change in how we express our love. Some women actually prefer this platinum power passion as now they and their partners have time to linger with no deadlines to fulfil or children to look after, and the whole question of pregnancy is taken out of the equation. Also, since some men may need a little more time to build up to an erection, there can be plenty of enjoyable foreplay.

In a long-term relationship, it is very easy to settle into a regular routine that doesn't vary. There is reassurance in knowing what you both like; however, that can lead to predictability and even, dare I say it, boredom. Eventually one or other partner may start to yearn for the earlier thrills in the relationship and feel unfulfilled. If there is hesitation or resistance around talking about this situation, then this can affect intimacy, which may lead down a slippery slope to bigger problems.

TIPS TO TRY

There are lots of ways to spice things up easily. The power of music, dressing up, exotic food; not forgetting location, location, location. Many of my clients are continually amazed at how even the slightest effort of creativity on their part reaps an unbelievable reaction from their partners. Think about it as an opportunity to use your creative skills in an important area of your life regularly. I'm not particularly talking about sex toys or gadgets – but if that what works for you, then why not? Experiment with lovemaking in a different room, on the kitchen table, in the bath or shower. The main thing is that creativity enhances your love together – it cannot replace it. Remember that sometimes the sexiest thing to do is simply to lie down side by side fully clad and look into each other's eyes.

Let your partner know that you are open to trying out new ways to express your love. Keep it quite simple: a new nightie or silk dressing gown could be a visual sign that tonight is the night; a caress or hug using the sense of touch to convey that you are open to lovemaking; suggestive whispers or sexting beforehand; the suggestion of a bath together later on can act as a sure-fire aphrodisiac. Be imaginative! You know your partner, so invent something that will appeal to them and their sense of romance.

OWNING UP TO AND OVERCOMING MISTAKES

An amazing woman told me that her husband had confessed to a brief dalliance abroad on a business trip.* It was over but he felt so guilty he wanted to tell her everything. She was devastated and felt betrayed and very hurt. We worked

---

* Details are changed for confidentiality.

together for a few sessions and she had a major breakthrough when she admitted that she was not the most ardent lover and, in fact, avoided it when she could. She did love her husband but she began to see that she was leaving out a very important aspect of their lives. In truth she had never really owned her sexuality and, although comfortable with her body size, she was not in her feminine power. It frightened her. Wisely realising that change was needed, she read about it and discussed it openly and frankly with me as her counselling psychotherapist. Slowly she began to introduce, little by little, new ways to express her love for her husband. It rocked her world and his. They are like newlyweds, much to the amazement of their family who to this day have no idea why.

CREATIVITY

Genes will out as we age; they can't lie. Our DNA code is imprinted with our parents and ancestors' ways of being. Some of my siblings and I love craftwork (such as knitting and crochet), reading avidly, gardening and storytelling. All hugely present in my mother's family. I also share with other family members a love of photography, dancing, opera music and collecting bric-a-brac. These were all part of my father's family's interests. My younger sisters, because our grandparents had passed away before they were born, never witnessed them actually do these hobbies; however, as they matured into adulthood, they found that they too had a natural ability for the same pursuits and so discovered a great way to take time out. Of course, when I was younger, I thought the hobby choices that my elders had made were boring, stupid and even quaint. I suppose I now know what the younger generation in our family thinks of us!

TIPS TO TRY
Out of curiosity or sheer fun, make a note of your favourite pastimes and see if you are doing any of those enjoyed by

the elders in your family. You may need to ask the oldest person alive in your family. You can then note what your siblings are doing and check to see if there is a correlation with your parents, grandparents or ancestors' interests. Take it a step further and look at what the next generation is up to. It might give insights to a pastime that could be shared with a family member. I've seen ten-year-olds enjoy fishing with grandad and two older siblings look forward to a bridge game with friends as a way of keeping in touch. Don't assume that being creative means that you have to write, play music or paint. How you lay a table, plant your herb garden or the type of books you read are all part of our creativity.

 WORDS OF WISDOM
Name: Sherrie Scott.
Country of origin: Northern Ireland.
Country of habitation: Rossnowlagh, Co. Donegal.
Age: Fifty-eight.
Occupation: Biomagnetic therapist.
1. What do you wish you had done or started earlier in your life?
I wish I had developed my own creative art practice earlier, rather than looking outside myself for teaching and direction. The journey of connecting to my own practice has shown me a way to give form to what's going on in my life. Keeping a little art book as part of my daily energy balance practice frees me up to experience colour and form in a non-judgemental way that nourishes my soul.
2. What are you delighted you did or started earlier in your life?
I am delighted that I had the good fortune to jump, swim, dive and run in the sea from the time I could walk. The sea element of water blesses me in its many forms and will always bring freshness and freedom to my life, whether I am looking at it or surrounded by it.

SENSE OF HUMOUR

For me a good sense of humour is vital to survive the vicissitudes of our modern world today. I truly love to see someone in their elder years having a good giggle. Somehow, I think they are showing their true colours by being able to laugh having made their way through the trials and tribulations of life. I enjoy wit, farce, puns, double entendres; in fact, most kinds of humour from visual gags that transcend language to clever long-winded, meandering stories that repeat a hilarious thread throughout. Having spent years working as a holistic therapist I really believe that laughter is the best medicine. It relieves tension, provides an outlet for release of pent-up emotions, connects people and naturally produces happy endorphins in the body. I could go on about the physiological advantages, but you get the picture and know what I mean. I think this is why many older people shared with me the importance of being with their young grandchildren. You can't be in the company of toddlers for very long without laughing at their antics. They live in the moment and grasp as much fun from it as they can – such a tonic for us adults.

TIPS TO TRY

If you recognise that you are not laughing as much as you could be or have lost your ability to enjoy life fully, do not despair. There are lots of ways of rediscovering this side of yourself. Awareness is the first step. Perhaps you need to offload some earlier life experiences that are dragging you down. Do a quick check and see if the people you hang out with are laugh inducing or stifling. If they are the latter, then why are you spending time with them? Hopefully you are not married to them; however, if you are, then here's a simple tip that works and might open up your relationship in a new way. Find out their favourite comedy, buy a box set and watch the series with them. The commonality of sharing laughter together over the same antics on the screen could start the ball rolling on communication in other ways. I had a seminal moment when some of my sisters gave me a voucher for a holistic centre as a present. I mulled over which course to choose and as I read out the list, my sisters said, 'Oh, you should definitely do the "clowning" one!' Was I far too serious, taking the classic eldest sister thing too far? Rather than be upset, especially since they said it with kindness and a twinkle in their eyes, I became a clown for a day. Well, I laughed like I have never laughed before and started to change my demeanour with the family to a lighter, fun way of being.

SPIRITUALITY

Personally I think the older we get the more spiritual we become. Why? Well, my theory is that we reach the 'Is this it?' stage in our mid-forties and wonder what life is all about. So we either question the religion we may have been following *or* revisit the spiritual practices we were brought up with. We may take up a new spiritual perspective based on life experiences including the death of a loved one or personal illness. The older we get the more conscious we become of our mortality or indeed our immortality, depending on what we believe in. We may have been very surprised at older relatives who professed to be staunch atheists all their lives but asked for a priest, pastor or rabbi at their deathbed.

It took me a long time to figure out what was best for me. I know that there are many paths to whatever you call God or Goddess or Spirit, and the eclectic mix that is shamanism suits me. It encompasses union of mind, body and soul with a love of nature and the seasons, a simple embracing of living in the present and a deep knowing that everything is sacred and has a soul. Life has its challenges but I have a toolkit of beliefs to help deal with them as I learn and grow.

I believe that my reason for being born at this time has changed over the years. It used to be to figure out who I am, then it was to see if I could love myself as I love others, and now it is to teach and encourage others to find their own path whatever that might be.

TIPS TO TRY

Imagine that when we die we have an opportunity to review our lives. Not a big scary thing with celestial judges but a personal review. How would we do? Would you regret not saying sorry to someone? Would you be sad that you didn't forgive and move on from an old grievance? Would you wish you had loved more? Embraced life fully? Slowed down to smell the roses? Now is the time to do this review. Don't leave it until it is too late. There is always enough time to be who we truly were born to be. If there was a purpose for you to be on earth as a human, what would your main function be? Perhaps to be a 'good enough' mother or father, to learn humility or to overcome a difficult challenge. Trust you will know.

WORDS OF WISDOM

Name: Ann Slevin.

Country of origin: Ireland.

Country of habitation: I immigrated to Sydney, Australia ten years ago.

Age: Seventy-seven.

Occupation: Secretary, mother of five, homemaker. I worked part-time and am now a holistic therapist and artist.

1. What do you wish you had done or started earlier in your life?

I wish I had taken time to love myself. It used to be selfish to put yourself first. Mothers tend to put themselves last. It is the old way now. I had to learn this by going out and doing holistic workshops. I wish I had known about it earlier. Even teenagers should know about this.

2. What are you delighted you did or started earlier in your life?

What stands to me now is working on the spiritual and feeding the soul. As I get older, to find an inner peace through meditation to connect with my inner knowing. I started meditating in Ireland but I always went to quiet places as a child. I had that connection with myself even then. I love the simplicity and spiritual connection that indigenous culture has to the land and every living creature. We are returning to this at this time on earth.

MRS O'BRIEN'S DOCTOR

I once met a charming doctor who asked me if I could guess how many hours he had spent on bedside manner in his medical training. He had studied about thirty years ago and the answer was zero hours. At the time this troubled him. One evening on an overnight shift he was trying to catch up on some much-needed sleep after a hectic day. His bleeper went off at 3 a.m. and the matron rang to say that Mrs O'Brien was asking for him. Groggily by phone he questioned the matron on how Mrs O'Brien was doing. The reply was that her blood pressure was normal, her drip in place, everything seemed to be fine. In fact the matron couldn't detect anything wrong. So, this young intern asked her to tell the patient that he would see her first thing in the morning and to go back to sleep.

The next day during the hospital rounds my friend was pulled aside by the top consultant professor and asked how the previous night had gone. The young intern gave an account of the shift but didn't even mention Mrs O'Brien since he thought the incident was inconsequential. After listening quietly for a few moments, the professor asked if he had heard from any of the older patients in the night, specifically Mrs O'Brien? My friend blushed and said he had and, satisfied that she was in no danger, he had sent a message that she should go back to sleep. The professor nodded sagely and replied, 'Your patient Mrs O'Brien is an old woman who woke up in the night alone and afraid. She needed the reassurance from you, her physician, at her bedside that she would be fine and live until the next day.'

'But', spluttered the young doctor, 'nobody told me that is what I was supposed to do.'

'Ah,' replied the professor, 'it's called common sense and compassion and you learn it from your elders. I am happy to pass on this very important piece of knowledge to you today.'

What a lesson! This doctor has become a wonderful example to his colleagues and he now makes sure to pass on this precious information to his juniors.

JUST BREATHE

Do you ever succumb and let the 'small stuff' bother you? At the simplest of glitches, it is so easy to become frustrated. Then we fail to see the big picture – the full perspective. The easiest way of calming our system down is to just *breathe*. Amazingly, our body is hardwired to listen to the call for calm and react accordingly. You can learn these wonderful techniques in yoga, t'ai chi classes, mindfulness or meditation workshops. However, just slow, deep breathing for three or four minutes will suffice. This is one of the oldest and most effective exercises to bring a sense of peace back to our nervous systems and works wonders in a short amount of time – no equipment needed.

TIPS TO TRY

Sit or lie down and bring your full attention (or as much as you can at the time) to your normal breath. Merely witness it, not changing or judging it in any way. Observe the air passing through your nostrils. When you have noticed that, shift your attention further down your body and see if you can feel your chest rise and fall as you breathe rhythmically in and out. Finally, bring your focus to your abdomen (below your navel) and note if it moves, even slightly, indicating that your breath has naturally deepened, filling your lungs fully and causing your diaphragm (a large flap of muscle below your lung cavity) to move up and down, which in turn affects your abdomen. This sends clear messages through your nervous system up to the brain, which results in calming the body and subsequently the mind. All this is naturally and simply achieved, while giving your mind the opportunity to observe something other than any problems, worries or frustrations.

Chapter Eleven   RETIREMENT

PLANNING AHEAD

What comes to mind when you hear the word 'retirement'–
left on the shelf, game over or free time at last? As we spiral
back to this topic, I'm guessing there are plenty of times
when you sit in traffic or slave away at your desk and dream
of eternal holidays and lots of time to yourself. Eventually
this will happen when you reach the age to, decide to or are
encouraged to finish your formal working life. Retirement
can be all your dreams come true *or* it can be very scary and
stressful, depending on how much you identify with your
career. You might be laughing loudly here, especially if you
are in your forties but do you have a pension fund? See, you
have actually started the planning already so why not take it a
step further? Retirement doesn't have to be a time of slowing
down. It can be a new growth spurt. It's just another phase of
life. Many of us envy people who retire early, perhaps thinking
they have some magical gift and must know some secret that
the rest of us have missed out on. Not necessarily so.

A DIFFERENT VIEWPOINT

I'm going to turn the concept of retirement on its head. I
have no intention of retiring since at the moment I actually
live as though I am retired. I love what I do passionately and
don't plan to stop until I have to. I used to work 9 a.m. to
5 p.m., sitting in traffic for ages to commute there and back.

I decided that there must be another way to live. Now I work mostly from home, seeing two or three clients a week. I used to regularly teach weekend courses with my husband in beautiful countryside locations, now we work mostly online since our energy levels have changed and all that travelling and moving about doesn't suit us anymore. All my @drkarenwardtherapist Workshops and Moon Mná Women's Circles are also online, which works well for those with small children, as the participants don't require babysitters. A few times a year I teach at home and abroad in gorgeous places.

I thought about all the things I used to dream about doing and I do them now while I am about to turn sixty. I meditate and do some yoga stretches on waking and potter in our little yard after breakfast. I walk in the Phoenix Park or up and down the Liffey most days. I see friends a couple of times a week. During 'term' time I do a class as a hobby, which over the years has included dancing, crafting, singing and now learning Irish. I holiday three times a year with at least two of these in Ireland, as I am conscious of the environment. I have no children, which means I could do this earlier in life than if I did have young dependants; however, I do know other couples who live as though they are retired and have teenagers. It is a state of mind really. Some of you could say, 'Karen, that's rubbish. You are still working.' And yes, I am, but at a retirement level, not at full tilt like I used to. Contrary to what you may think, I don't have a massive nest egg and haven't won a big lottery yet. I still pay all my bills very comfortably with my husband, who has a similar version of my lifestyle with different hobbies and interests but at the same pace.

I live very well as I use my talents and resources to the maximum. For example, as a necessary part of my training after qualifying as a holistic therapist I worked in a leisure centre. I met lots of fabulous clients who I didn't have to find and attract to my clinic – they were already there. Naturally, I paid the centre for this privilege and the therapy space.

Since then I built up a reputation so that I could work from my home clinic in my own space and people travelled to see me. Now I have changed my working life again; I see a small number of clients online and most of my work is teaching or supervising others – again online. We share a wonderful virtual assistant and she does a lot of administration with a strong marketing role too. What I am saying essentially is be wiser as you grow older. Decide how you want to live your life and then find a way to make it happen, eventually. You may need the help of a career coach to fine-tune your plans.

DON'T BE AFRAID OF CHANGE

Some of us may be fearful of retirement as a huge life change foisted upon us at a vulnerable time in our lives. Nobody is trying to hurt or belittle you in any way. It is simply a part of a natural life cycle, just like pruning the garden or clearing up the older leaves to allow the young shoots come forward in time. Some babies walk at one year, some at ten months and some at fourteen months. There is nothing right or wrong about the timing, just the individual coming forward to advance when they are ready. It is the same with retirement except this time we may not have the choice to go when we want; therefore, we need to make sure we are prepared for it.

So address any fears now in a monitored way with help and advice from people who are in the know. They may offer you some consultancy work or freelance cover for sick or maternity leave within the company after you have retired. They will probably suggest joining some associations or clubs so that you still have an active social element in your life. One of the biggest changes upon retirement is the lack of a routine and interaction with others. Most of us have been members of groups of people all our lives, so why should it be any different after retirement?

TIPS TO TRY
Retirement is not about sitting at home on the shelf anymore, unless of course you want it to be that way. You have a choice. Most large companies have fabulous courses offered by the human resources department to prepare you for retirement. It is well worth attending one of these at around fifty rather than waiting until the last minute at sixty-six years of age. The Retirement Planning Council of Ireland (www.rpc.ie) offer courses from €530, with a couple's version at €795, covering finance, healthy living, social welfare entitlements amongst other relevant topics. Check whether your company offers free courses that you can sign up for early to plan ahead.

HAVE A PLAN

You can draw up exciting lists for the things you always wanted to do in life now. Imagine a boring day filing when you can daydream of visiting Paris, learning to canoe, painting a landscape, whatever. This is the time to harness your energy, to get motivated and stimulate yourself and friends for new challenges. An aunt of mine is invited back to the company she worked in every year to meet all the other retirees for lunch and catch up on the company news. It is a chance to socialise in a supportive environment with people she had known for many working years. An inspired and thoughtful move by that large company.

INVENT YOUR OWN WORK

We are creatures of habit whether we admit it or not and we thrive best on a regular routine. After you retire there is bound to be a period of delicious lie ins and pyjama days. Quite soon, however, you will need to invent a new routine, otherwise you could easily fall into the trap of having too much time to think, which can lead to the early stages of depression if you are prone to feeling low in yourself. An easy way to combat this is to ask yourself what you have always wanted to do. Something that expands your social network and/or challenges you mentally. Try out a few things that you think you might like to get the proverbial ball rolling, then expand your horizons further.

TIPS TO TRY
Consider at retirement taking a gap year, just like some leaving certificate students, to travel widely and visit the places you have dreamt about.

Maybe the hobby you let go when you juggled children, a career and a relationship, is worth having a look at again but with fresh eyes.

You could take the opportunity to turn your hobby into your second job. Now that we are living longer, we may all have the opportunity to have two careers in our lifetime. The 'main' job after school or college, and our 'retirement' job. These will be much more relaxed and there probably won't be as much pressure to perform or earn a certain amount to pay the mortgage. Remember that although you might think how wonderful it will be to retire and at last do nothing, the majority of wealthy people fundraise or keep busy in some way to give purpose to their lives – so a hobby of golf may morph into inventive ways to pay for a new clubhouse or going to yoga class could mean deciding to learn to teach it. Perhaps you could keep mentally alert by coaching the local junior soccer team. Enjoy this exciting time in your life – you've earned it.

INTENTION
If you think about it, for most of our lives we have had a focused intention to our days. This would have been originally to become educated (to whatever level was available to us then), forming relationships, carrying out a job either inside or outside the home, etc. There is a beautiful wise saying 'energy follows thought'; in other words, what you think about

becomes your reality. This is true if we ruminate and spiral into sadness over the old 'shoulda, coulda, woulda' scenarios and also if we hold a positive can-do attitude to retirement. So, be mindful of what you constantly think about – this is the reason why you read or hear about the importance of staying positive and proactive.

WORDS OF WISDOM
Name: M. O'Grady.
Country of origin and of habitation: Ireland.
Age: Ninety-three.
Occupation: Farmer's wife.
1. What do you wish you had done or started earlier in your life?
I have eight children and rearing them took all my time. I joined the ICA (Irish Countrywomen's Association). Maybe I left too soon as I thought the children needed me. I wish I had stayed in it for social reasons.
2. What are you delighted you did or started earlier in your life?
I travelled over Europe and visited the Holy Lands, Fatima and Lourdes. I now enjoy a holiday yearly in Lanzarote. During the recessions in the eighties and nineties my faith and the love of the Mother of God gave me hope and kept me going.

SOWING THE SEEDS FOR HOPE
We need to bring hope into our lives when we require it most – planning for our future. A good way to do this is to think about special times in the past when we felt hopeful and reflect on key elements that may now be repeated to good effect. This might be the company of certain people, being physically fit, having time or being blissfully occupied. These can be savoured and now if incorporated into our life again can help us to look forward with relish.

Our natural life force or energy means that as our birthright we have four major abilities – trust, love, wonder and humour. We all have these until we die. They never go away, but with the ups and downs of life they become clouded over as we lose touch with them, and even perhaps think that somehow we have missed out on them. If we can get back in touch with these inner abilities, we may solve the majority of our problems, including any nervousness about retirement, in a more effective way. We can help ourselves access these abilities very simply through our hobbies or interests.

TIPS TO TRY
Think about a favourite interest. Do you ever lose track of time when you do it? Do you worry? Do you have brainwaves or brilliant ideas during or when you are finished? Do you feel excited or happy as you prepare, and totally chilled out afterwards? Once we arrive at a relaxed state, often for the first time in months, suddenly the ability to think clearly and objectively is easier. Now we can harness all our resources, set new goals and make decisions with clarity. We need to remember that most of us haven't had the time, perhaps for years, for such so-called frivolities so now we may rediscover a past interest and see the merit of its benefits.

PROJECTS
The aim of this book is to show that it is never too early to prepare for old age, and I extend this to the retirement phase of our life too. I'm generalising now, but from my clinical work I have found that many men need projects to focus on throughout their lives. These may have been teenage sports, the start of a romance, work projects, a hobby or interest. Retirement can be very daunting when there is a huge gap in our usual daily routine. Many men talk about the boredom factor having a big impact on their self-esteem. Preparation is the key for this phase of life, when you will have no set schedule

and a lot of extra hours on your hands. Again, I generalise here but women often have more diverse interests during their working years, so retirement may not be as big a change.

REVITALISE YOUR RELATIONSHIPS

Women unite! Men unite! Join a golf, bowling or bridge club. Why? Let's take golf as an example – for two hours you get to focus on a little white ball to the exclusion of all your worries or cares, while in the fresh air, getting exercise in the community of women or men at the same phase of life. It's a win-win situation. That is, of course, if you actually like golf.

Choose an interest that excites you. Camaraderie with fellow retirees is very important, so you don't feel you are the only one on the planet going through this. It is also a time to form new friendships while getting out of the house and exploring fresh things to do.

WORDS OF WISDOM
Name: Breda Kelly.
Country of origin: Tipperary, Ireland.
Country of habitation: Wexford, Ireland.
Age: Eighty-nine.
Occupation: Hotelier and company director of Kelly's Resort Hotel and Spa, Rosslare, mother of seven.
1. What do you wish you had done or started earlier in your life?
I wish I was a good swimmer. I feel it would have stood to me later in life.
2. What are you delighted you did or started earlier in your life?
I took up bridge and still play today. It keeps my mind active and it is very sociable too.

Chapter Twelve　　　　　LOSS AND BEREAVEMENT

GRIEVING

There are three absolute certainties in life – birth, change and death – and many of us are terrified of one if not all of them. When we grieve, we are dealing with all three at the same time – the death of a loved one, the huge change that brings and, depending on your beliefs, the birth of their new transition to spirit. In olden times, there were very specific rituals and ceremonies to help the whole grieving process. In our modern world many of these have been lost. Nowadays if we don't follow a formal religious path, there is a gap that we may yearn to fill, to ease the pain and suffering to acceptance and peace. We sometimes forget that death is a part of life and we encounter mini-deaths all the time; for example, finishing school, leaving a job or ending a relationship. Physical death is a larger more final version of these. I often think that if we are afraid of death, what it actually means is that we are afraid of life itself.

Imagine living every day as though it was your last, wringing out every last drop of excitement, love and friendship. In truth none of us know when we will die for certain so in the face of that big change we might as well live life as best we can. If this was your last day on earth, how would you live it, what would you say, who would you spend it with?

BELIEF SYSTEMS

I'm guessing that some of you will not like reading this chapter. If that is the case, I would highly recommend you do because you very probably need this information the most. We all will die someday and so will our family and friends; therefore, we might as well get used to the concept and make peace with the inevitable in preparation. Let's look at this factually for a moment.

Either:
1. We die and that's it. We won't know any pain or pleasure. We will just be gone, simply stop living – that's not so bad, is it?

or:
2. We die and according to our belief system – a particular religious or spiritual practice – we go to Heaven or Nirvana or Valhalla or the Otherworld or some other spiritual realm where our soul continues in a good way. Doesn't that ease our minds? After all, if we take our beliefs to heart then all will be well and we'll pass on to a beautiful place.

Yet somehow that's not always how we think about death and there is still a lot of fear about it. As a counselling psychotherapist for many years, hearing lots of people's perceptions, I think the trepidation comes from two places: a) we feel we will be judged or sent to somewhere awful like hell; or b) we are left behind and physically ache for those who have passed away, missing them and their presence with us. With the former, if you feel your life will be judged by a spiritual deity of your belief system, then it makes sense to change your life now. Make amends, say you are sorry, love and give yourself a clean slate. For the latter, we need to realise that bereavement is a fact of life and can bring many joys and blessings along with the sorrow and grief.

THE OLD WAYS

In Ireland up to about eighty years ago, there was a very healthy attitude to death. The funeral ceremony was preceded by a 'wake', which was a life celebration of the loved one who had passed. The expression 'waking the dead' meant rousing the soul of those who had died to their birth in a new spiritual home. Their favourite food and drink would be served, and their family and friends all came to celebrate their life with stories, song and even dance. In the midst of all this the open casket displayed their body for all to see, including the children. The reason was that everyone could pay their respects but also see clearly that their soul or life force had left their body and gone to a place of eternal rest. This started the whole grieving process as people could see that their loved one had moved on. Often an integral part of the wake was the presence of keeners (*na caoineadh* in Irish Gaelic), a group of women who were professional 'criers' dressed in black. During the evening they would sit in the corner, wail, cry and moan to help the family voice their pain, especially for those who might find it more difficult to cry.

Then the neighbours stepped in to look after the grieving family, preparing the food and keeping an eye on them for a month afterwards. At the month's mind it was time for the family to start looking after themselves. Finally, at the year anniversary the grieving process was deemed to be over. If it wasn't, then there was something out of balance and more counselling from the priest was needed to help the family move on.

TIPS TO TRY

It can be very helpful to create your own version of a keening ceremony. Pick a time when you are alone or with a trusted friend or family member. Make sure you are not in a hurry and will not be disturbed. Put on a really weepy film to play the part of the keeners for you. Basically, any film with a sad storyline will do. Many men find the old-fashioned film *The Champ* with young John Voight works very well. As you watch, have some tissues nearby and give yourself full permission to cry for the characters on the screen. When the film ends, sit there and allow yourself to think of the person who has passed away and emote. It may be appropriate to have their photo or some special mementos present – trust you will know what is best. It might feel good to write about your feelings and emotions as another form of release. Take as much time as you need. The film will have started the process for you and now you can let nature take its course until you feel you have released enough for that time. You can always repeat this again if you feel the need.

STAGES OF BEREAVEMENT

Many of those who work with the bereaved notice that there are certain patterns to the stages of grief. Dr Elisabeth Kübler-Ross, a Swiss psychiatrist, wrote many books on this sensitive subject including the classic *On Death and Dying* where she outlined her model of the five stages of grief – denial, anger, bargaining, depression and finally acceptance. Others who work with death and dying have noted and written about other stages, and indeed it is different for everybody. They don't always happen in the same order or length of time for everyone.

When someone we love passes away the first sense is often one of shock. This occurs even if the person is old and has lived a good life but is hugely heightened if they are young or die suddenly. Our bodies experience numbness and we don't know what to do or say. Usually, we are catapulted into the organisational aspect of spreading the word and making the funeral arrangements. This has the effect of keeping us occupied and postpones our grief initially. This phase is often followed by exhaustion after all the busyness and being on view very publicly during our loved one's ceremonies. Denial can often manifest when we hope, and often pretend, that the death hasn't actually happened. This is sometimes poignantly felt when we wake up a few days later and forget that our loved one has passed away.

Many of us don't actually know how to be in a death situation. It is a shocking and tragic time, and nowadays we aren't taught how to behave since many people don't like to talk about death anymore. We want to join the world again, but when we do we can feel like we don't belong. Trust your intuition. You will know when you are ready to go back to work or out socially. We need to go through the pain of death to come out the other side. You might think you're going crazy, not knowing if you are doing the grieving process the right way. Everyone goes through a version of this feeling. Bereavement counsellors can help you through this difficult time. Some emotions may surprise you, like the anger stage. This may be directed towards yourself, the hospital or even your perception of God. Know that it is perfectly fine to express and release the anger, without feeling guilty. Change will come.

TIPS TO TRY

When someone close to you dies it is a special time to go within and feel your feelings. Be good to yourself. Listen to your body. Run a long bath, light candles and have a warming soak in nourishing essential oils: rose for well-being, lavender for relaxation and chamomile for calm. You may not feel like eating much, so soups are a great nourishing, easy food at this time. Cuddle a pillow wrapped in their clothing and let the tears come, let the mourning sounds out. It's good to cry.

WORDS OF WISDOM
Name: Justin Fitzgerald.
Country of origin: Ireland.
Country of habitation: Ireland.
Age: Forty-eight.

Occupation: A barber since leaving school and I was happy to open my own barber shop fifteen years ago, which is still going strong.

1. What do you wish you had done or started earlier in your life?

I wish I hadn't started to smoke when I was younger. I regret that it is now part of my work environment with the lads who all smoke too. I am conscious about it and only smoke in the garden at home using mouth spray freshener. My girls don't smoke, thankfully. I am at a loss at how to quit now.

2. What are you delighted you did or started earlier in your life?

I married the fabulous girl I met at fifteen years of age and we have two beautiful daughters we are so proud of – my pride and joy!

IT'S ALL ABOUT YOU

Depending on how you look at it, the person who has passed away is either gone for good and out of pain, or in a loving spiritual place. The grieving process is all about *you* coming to terms with their passing. It is easy to get stuck in the fear, guilt or helplessness of the situation. Our mind can play tricks and spin into negative spirals of depression and self-depreciation. We've all heard the expression 'time will heal' and probably feel like screaming at the person who has said it – but it is actually true. There is a reason that core grieving takes a full year at least.

Confusion is a big part of it too. One day you feel back to normal and the next day, the smallest memory can trigger waves of sadness. Each life event is a milestone; for example, birthdays and holidays. Sometimes it is a good idea to change family traditions, such as going away for the next Christmas rather than trying to celebrate with an empty place at the table. Though for many families it is better to go through the normal rituals and include the happy memories of Dad carving the turkey or Mum making her special cake. Everyone grieves differently so whatever you are doing is the right way for you to do it. Just remember to respect other family members' methods of grieving.

TIPS TO TRY
A little bit of quiet time can ground you, giving a sense of connection. Light a candle and talk to your loved one the way you always did. Tell them about your day and what's going on and wish them well wherever you perceive them to be. Use your beliefs, whatever they are, to ask for help and guidance at this difficult time. If you are supporting someone in their grieving process, let them know you are there for them but give them the space to release their emotions in their own way. Your presence alone is hugely supportive; don't feel you have to find the 'right' words to show you care. Just be yourself and remember laughter is as much a relief as tears are.

A SENSE OF ACCEPTANCE
Somewhere in our life we will come to the point where we ask the question 'Where did we come from and where are we going?' Usually this happens around the time of bereavement. Spirituality is a very personal matter, even if we follow a formal religion. Many people talk about a sign they feel their loved one gives them to say that they have reached a happy place in the afterlife. Some talk of vivid dreams or coincidences, like favourite songs playing on the radio. Nature is a good place to nurture your own soul when grieving. When feeling low, seeing a tiny bud in the depths of winter gives a feeling of hope, even after despair. A huge part of the difficulty in grief is the loss of communication with our loved one, which leaves a gaping hole in our lives. Talking to a spiritual presence, such as Mother Mary or a beloved pet, can help hugely too.

PREPARING FOR OUR OWN TIME

Now I know this sounds very morbid but it shouldn't be. Many of us have a family plot in the local graveyard, so this is just an extension of that concept of preparation. My husband and I have bought our matching plot in a new woodland burial site and have pre-purchased our eco willow caskets so our family don't have to choose what to put us in when we are gone.

Now think of the pile of clutter you may have in your house. You know what I'm talking about – the bulging spare room, attic or extra wardrobe. You probably wince every time you pass it and think you'll get around to it someday. I imagine you love your nearest and dearest very much. If you don't sort out your affairs now then you are leaving it to them after you have gone. Think of the difficulty of grieving *and* having to try to find a will, bank account books and house deeds, never mind clearing your clutter too. Sort it out now!

TIPS TO TRY
Make sure to leave your will in a place that key people in your family know about, with a letter specifying the type of ceremony you would like. Too often weeks after the cremation, letters are found hidden away expressing a wish to be buried in a specific place when the ashes have already been scattered. I know someone who wanted her friends to celebrate her life in bright colours at a jolly lunch before her burial, which was a lovely idea. But it wasn't very realistic since everyone was in deep grief and not ready to celebrate yet. Also, the funeral directors and crematorium had a specific time rota and so could not delay for lunch arrangements. In the end we all waited a few months and had the exact celebration she would have wanted then.

I LOVE YOUS AND I FORGIVE YOUS

This concept blew me away. Think of your life today. Is there anyone you need to forgive for anything? So often in my clinic I meet people who are distraught years after someone has died, because they didn't express their emotions and tell family and friends that they loved them or that they were sorry. It is called 'living cleanly'. Meaning that you live life as you mean to die – with all your affairs in order and saying all the things you mean to say to those who you care deeply about. It's a good way to be. If for some reason you are terrified of the thought of someone close to you dying, then process this now with a close friend, a counsellor or someone who has been through it and understands.

Any hospice staff member or palliative carer will tell you that frequently people die alone as it is easier to slip away with no emotional ties present. A family may have been holding a bedside vigil for weeks or months. Then when someone goes off for a much-needed five-minute break, guess what? Mammy slips away peacefully. Now in our human mind we think how sad it is that she died all alone. What we are not taking into account is that Mammy probably had a whole host of her ancestors and spiritual helpers with her to guide her off to her new life. Much easier than if her family were crying and begging for her not to leave. As I said, grieving is all about us, not the person who is free of this world and exploring the next.

TIPS TO TRY

We can project onto a loved one our fears and trepidations, whereas they are probably ready to go. Don't be nervous of talking to someone who is ill about death. They may be waiting for someone to bring the subject up. A visit from the hospital chaplain or local priest, pastor or rabbi will, of course, make this easier depending on their beliefs. Whispering something like this could be helpful: 'It's okay to slip away now, Dad. We will miss you but we'll be fine.

We know it is your time to leave and we wish you well and a peaceful passing.' This can be just what they need – permission to die knowing that the family will be alright when the natural grieving is over. Consider doing this a few times, especially if someone is in a coma and hanging on though they seem to be ready to go. It has an amazing effect and can often ensure that family are present around the time of death since this very beautiful gesture can mean fairly imminent departure for the ill person.

AN HONOUR
I was truly honoured to be at the deathbed of a great woman. She had had cancer for over eighteen years and this was the fourth time it had come back. After the first two years, she said the amazing words, 'I'm glad I got cancer. It has taught me so much about how to live.' Wasn't her insight incredible? She certainly showed her family and friends how to live, but she really showed us all how to die. Her time in the hospice was one of respect, dignity, laughter and immense love. In fact, she summed it all up by saying to me, 'Karen, in the end, love is all there is.' What a beautiful memory and life lesson she gave me to treasure.

MAKING A DIFFERENCE – LEAVING A LEGACY
So how do you want to be remembered? As a kind person who lived life to the full? Do you want to honour all your family fairly in your will not just with money but in the well-chosen gifts you may bestow on them, such as items of furniture and certain classic clothes? I treasure my dad's schoolbook, my granny's crystal sugar bowl and my grandad's chess set. You may want to leave a living legacy behind you for the cats and dogs' home or a particular charity that is dear to your heart.

TIPS TO TRY
There are ways of leaving your mark on the world by loving as much as you can, by being an inspiration to others in even the smallest of ways. Sit down and have a think about what you have left behind already. If it is not enough for you, then be creative! A simple yet highly effective way to know you are on track with this is to attempt to write your own epitaph in a light-hearted way. What would you like people to say about you when it is your time to go? When you have figured out what it is, then make sure you are living your life in that way right now.

WORDS OF WISDOM
Name: Marie Meade.
Country of origin: Kerry, Ireland.
Country of habitation: London, England and now Kerry, Ireland.
Age: Sixty-eight.
Occupation: Financial advisor.
1. What do you wish you had done or started earlier in your life?
I wish I had started yoga years ago in my younger life. I was fifty and moved back home to Ireland from England when I began, but I could have made room for it earlier. However, I was busy with a career in banking and raising our family in London.
2. What are you delighted you did or started earlier in your life?
My husband and I are very pleased we moved back to Kerry in our fifties. We really are enjoying rural living and the slow pace of life.

Chapter Thirteen   CONCLUSION

WHAT ARE THE SECRETS OF AGELESS AGEING?
As we approach the end of this book, we reflect on what we have learned about the precious secrets of ageless ageing and longevity. In the chapter 'Midlife Opportunity', we realised the positive potential of the third phase of our lives without the responsibility or need to provide for others where we can reinvent ourselves boldly. Fulfilling our dreams is within our remit. The next two chapters, 'Physicality' and 'Our Magnificent Bodies', both taught us the importance of looking after our body, the house of our souls, wisely. This is a huge investment in our future. No point in having an active mind excited to explore new opportunities with a body that can't handle the pace. Prevention is indeed the best medicine. With 'Relationships' we learnt how we can reinvent our partnerships and friendships with fresh perspective – no need to stagnate. Love truly is all there is and there are many forms of it available to us. In 'Choices' we focused on how to say no to both people and situations as we, perhaps for the first time, say yes to our wants and desires. As we continued on to 'Society's View of Old Age', we recognised that both women and men pass through an energetic shift, a portal if you will, as we reach our crone and sage years and the requirement for rites of passage.

Ageing is a holistic phenomenon, both physical and psychological, and with the chapter 'Mental Adjustment' we saw the need to come to terms with balancing our thoughts, both positive and negative, as well as pacifying our critical eye. Next the 'Wisdom' chapter really brought us to a place of embracing the innate understandings we have gleaned from our life experience to date. In 'New Ways of Being' we acknowledged our ability to carry on all we have absorbed from our foremothers and forefathers, while releasing that which no longer serves us. How vital a sense of humour is was revealed in 'Holistic Viewpoint' as we contemplated our spirituality, however that may translate in our lives. With 'Retirement' we consciously looked at the importance of preparation, as we sow the seeds for hope in the future. 'Loss and Bereavement' brought us to a place of acceptance and building a legacy for others to carry on.

Now we reflect on all the treasures we have gathered. Some of you may have found solace in recognising everything that you already know and have in place, others may be surprised at some of the more obvious or seemingly innocuous suggestions that you may have missed. I trust that everyone will have gained perspective and revel in the connotations of excitement and freedom this stage of life brings.

This beautifully evocative poem by Sophie Hannah says it all. We have to start now while we can.

Now and Then
'Now that I'm fifty-seven,'
my mother used to say,
'Why should I waste a minute?
Why should I waste a day
Doing the things I ought to
simply because I should?
Now that I'm fifty-seven
I'm done with that for good.'
But now and then I'd catch her
trapped in some thankless chore
just as she might have been at
fifty-three or fifty-four

And I would want to say to her
(and I have to bite my tongue)
that if you mean to learn a skill
it's well worth starting young
And so, to make sure I'm in time
for fifty, I've begun
to do exactly as I please
now that I'm thirty-one.*

WORDS OF WISDOM

I endeavoured to talk to people from very different walks of life to gain a wide perspective of how old age is viewed. I was really struck that most of those in their eighties and nineties had little or no regrets. Is this something that happens as you age and have contemplated your life? Do we become more philosophical as we age? It seems that we do. I know some of the interviewees personally and they have had far from a charmed existence. Perhaps because of these difficulties, they have come to terms with what life has given them and how they have coped. Many talked about the importance of a good communicative relationship, a way of nurturing their soul, time to pursue creative interests and a love of nature.

I was surprised to hear time and time again of those who wished they had travelled more. Perhaps they lived in a time when airplane journeys were still exotic and expensive. Indeed, for many, travel meant emigration from necessity and not the holidays we can easily go on nowadays. I imagine that they heard about the broadening minds of the ones who did have that experience.

I enjoyed hearing about those who were very happy to have had their children early. I wonder how the current generation, who are statistically having their children later in life after academic years, will answer in years to come. It was poignant to hear some of the older women speak of giving up so much to rear their children. Thankfully now that times

* Sophie Hannah, *Selected Poems*, London: Penguin Carcanet Press Ltd., 2013.

have changed and our menfolk are stepping in to co-parent that would ameliorate the situation hugely.

How do we do more than survive but thrive throughout the ageing process? The so-called fountain of youth is how we live and look after ourselves, indeed our attitude to life, and is not found in some expensive cream. If we eat healthily five days a week, exercise for an hour three or four times a week and have a way to relax with love in our lives, then we have the secret of longevity. It's that simple and has a scientific basis too. Your body is a bit like a snail's shell, it houses our mind and soul. We alone have the responsibility to look after it. Remember not even the richest person in the world can pay someone to eat, sleep or exercise for them. The more we look after our bodies, the easier it is to maintain good health and reap the benefits of looking our best.

IMMORTALITY

Do you want to be immortal? If you believe our soul lives on, then you are immortal already. However, you may want to leave a living legacy behind you. I consider this book my version. I hope it inspires you, the reader. I also hope that the people I teach spread the holistic way of being to any family, friends and community who are interested. There are ways of leaving your mark on the world by loving as much as you can, by being an inspiration to others in even the smallest of ways.

'To be young, really young, takes a very long time.'
Pablo Picasso

MY OWN WORDS OF WISDOM

Name: Karen Ward.

Country of origin: Dublin, Ireland.

Country of habitation: Dublin and often West Cork, Ireland.

Age: Fifty-nine.

Occupation: Counselling psychotherapist, teacher, supervisor, Irish Celtic shamanic therapist, writer, wife and friend.

1. What do I wish I had done or started earlier in my life?

I wish I had understood and come to appreciate and honour my femininity. As the eldest and a Capricorn, I was a serious child who loved school and went on to study science in college. I was very driven, left-brained, my active masculine side to the fore, and it wasn't until my late thirties when I discovered the bounty of holistic therapies that my world expanded greatly to gift me balance in my life, as I embraced the sensuality and still nature of my feminine side.

2. What am I delighted I did or started earlier in my life?

I am blessed to have reached a point in life where I could be open to, call in and receive the love of a good man who I am proud to call my husband. He encourages me, a strong woman, to pursue my dreams – to be the best that I can be. Through trial and error over the years, I have learnt to love myself, warts and all, eventually allowing me to begin and continue to fulfil my destiny while creating my legacy.

APPENDIX

HOLISTIC CLEANSE
Are you eating healthier, exercising more – or just thinking about it? 'If only I could motivate myself just to get started' is a familiar cry. Here is a very simple cleanse plan you can do in one week (and also extend if you wish to). We are not talking about a scary strict diet regime that will upset your metabolism and be hard to do. This is done in conjunction with your regular routine and three meals a day. A cleanse should be done for a limited period of time, ideally one or two weeks. After this you may incorporate some elements into your normal healthy eating and living, which is a sustainable way to maintain your good work.

A cleanse will detox your system to look and feel fantastic while boosting your energy levels and immune system, and it's not as hard as you think. Toxins are basically anything not natural to your body systems – smoke, pollution, food additives and processed colourings and flavourings. Over years they clog up your body, soak up all your natural energy, age your facial skin and drain away your motivation, leaving you feeling down. Sound familiar? The excellent side effects of cleansing are clearer skin, more energy, a flatter abdomen and it can help eradicate the dreaded cellulite.

I do a more in-depth two-week version of this every three months and others join me* as we support each other. This

* All details on my website: www.drkarenwardtherapist.ie/love-yourself-cleanse-challenge/

seven-day plan is an ideal start for both men and women. Check with your doctor if you are very overweight, have not exercised for six months or have any medical conditions.

Preparation is essential. You will need to shop for healthy food and plan your week. It is best to start at the weekend when you have time to rest and get used to the initial discomfort that indicates that the plan is working. (Note: There is no alcohol on this week-long cleanse so your social habits may need to be adjusted accordingly.) You may have as much water, herbal tea and fruit as you like.

You will need to buy: lemons, gluten-free porridge, bread, pasta and crackers, plenty of fruit and salad, protein such as fish, cheese (goat, sheep, vegan or organic cow), potatoes, brown rice, quinoa and different types of soup.

DAY 1 (Ideally a Saturday)
Feeling: Excited, motivated and ready

- Wake up at the same time every day (choose your normal weekday wake-up hour). Stretch yourself slowly. Hands up and toes down *or* pick a manageable stretch that you have learnt at a reputable class or from a physiotherapist.
- Drink some hot water with lemon (to 'shower' your internal system) as you prepare your breakfast of fruit and organic yogurt *or* fruit and porridge. Eat slowly.
- Keep yourself occupied in nice ways, such as visiting a food market, a museum or an art gallery, and your usual Saturday pursuits.
- Have a piece of fruit and an herbal tea at 11 a.m. Bring it in your bag.
- For lunch eat a salad (only vinaigrette dressing) with some protein like fish or cheese (goat, sheep, vegan or organic cow). This may be at home or at a restaurant.
- Do an exercise of your choice for an hour but make sure you warm up and cool down before and

afterwards. An aerobic exercise that gets the heart and lungs working (cycling, swimming, fast walking, running) would be good.

- For dinner eat two types of vegetable and some carbohydrate such as brown rice, boiled or baked potato or wholemeal pasta.
- Watch a feel-good movie and chill out.

DAY 2 (Ideally a Sunday)
Feeling: Headache, a few spots, sleepy

- Do two stretches.
- Drink your lemon hot water and eat your fruit and porridge.
- Do your usual Sunday pursuits or nice things to keep you occupied.
- Have your piece of fruit and herbal tea.
- For lunch have a similar meal to Saturday, eat a salad (only vinaigrette dressing) with some protein like fish or cheese (goat, sheep, vegan or organic cow). This may be at home or at a restaurant.
- Exercise for an hour. Snooze after if you need to.
- For dinner eat two types of vegetable and some carbohydrate such as brown rice, boiled or baked potato or wholemeal pasta.
- Soak in a warm bath for an hour with relaxing music playing nearby.
- Use essential oil of lavender to soothe and calm.

DAY 3 (Ideally first workday)
Feeling: Headache's over, still sleepy

- Do three stretches.
- Drink your lemon hot water and eat your fruit and porridge.
- Take it easy workwise if possible. Explain to colleagues that you are on a cleanse.

- Eat a piece of fruit and drink herbal tea. Bring a supply of your favourite fruit into work if necessary.
- For lunch a big bowl of healthy soup and two slices of wholemeal, gluten-free bread or crackers. (If your work canteen supplies a hot dinner, then swap your lunch until later.)
- Walk for half an hour either at lunchtime or directly after work.
- For dinner eat a salad and some protein (lean organic meat/fish/dairy).
- Potter then go to bed early with a fabulous new book or magazine.

DAY 4 (Workday)
Feeling: Still tired and spotty

- Do three stretches.
- Drink your lemon hot water and eat your fruit and porridge.
- Take it easy workwise; try not to schedule big meetings today.
- Eat a piece of fruit and drink herbal tea.
- For lunch a big bowl of healthy soup and two slices of wholemeal, gluten-free bread or crackers. (If your work canteen supplies a hot dinner, then swap this with lunch.)
- Walk for half an hour either at lunchtime or directly after work.
- For dinner eat a salad and some protein (lean organic meat/fish/dairy).
- Phone a friend or invite them around for a smoothie. Buy them or, if you are inclined, have fun and make one with an apple, celery and pear.

DAY 5 (Workday)
Feeling: Detox effects starting to wear off

- Do three stretches.
- Drink your lemon hot water and eat your fruit and porridge.
- Take it easy workwise if possible.
- Eat a piece of fruit and drink herbal tea.
- For lunch, either in or out, eat a salad with a vinaigrette dressing, with some protein like fish or cheese (goat, sheep, vegan or organic cow). (If your work canteen supplies a hot dinner, then swap this with lunch.)
- Walk for half an hour either at lunchtime or directly after work.
- For dinner eat two types of vegetable and some carbohydrate such as brown rice, boiled or baked potato or wholemeal pasta.
- Watch a feel-good movie or your favourite soap and chill out.

DAY 6 (Workday)
Feeling: More energised, in good form

- Do three stretches.
- Drink your lemon hot water and eat your fruit and porridge.
- Take it easy workwise.
- Eat a piece of fruit and drink herbal tea.
- For lunch, either in or out, eat a salad with a vinaigrette dressing, with some protein like fish or cheese (goat, sheep, vegan or organic cow). (If your work canteen supplies a hot dinner, then swap this with lunch.)
- Walk for half an hour either at lunchtime or directly after work.
- For dinner eat two types of vegetable and some carbohydrate such as brown rice, boiled or baked potato or wholemeal pasta.
- Do some extra exercise of your choice for an hour.

DAY 7 (Workday)
Feeling: Success, a full detox week nearly done

- Do three stretches.
- Drink your lemon hot water, eat your fruit and porridge.
- Work as usual but take it easy if possible.
- Eat a piece of fruit and drink herbal tea.
- For lunch, either in or out, try a gluten-free sandwich full of fresh salad items with either vegan cheese or egg. (Again if your work canteen supplies a hot dinner, then swap this with lunch.)
- Walk for half an hour either at lunchtime or directly after work.
- For dinner eat a protein (lean meat/fish/tofu) stir-fry with brown rice.
- Dance at home with a few friends or sing karaoke. Celebrate by drinking fancy homemade juice cocktails – non-alcoholic, of course.

Note: When you reach the day after your cleanse don't fall into the trap of overdoing it. Introduce some simple treats – a glass or two of good wine, one chocolate bar made from 70 per cent cocoa, or a slice of carrot cake.

FOLLOW-ON MAINTENANCE CLEANSE TIPS

1. Drink boiled water cooled with a squeeze of lemon in the morning to prepare your digestive system for the day and gently ease elimination of the previous day's food. This simple tip is great for your skin.
2. For two days at a time avoid red meat, salt, sugary foods (cakes, biscuits, sweets). If you do this one day on and one day off, it becomes easier since you are not going cold turkey. You will find after a week that you begin to notice the effect of this maintenance cleanse on your energy levels and this will motivate you to continue.

3. Drink at least the equivalent of three small bottles of still mineral water a day. Often headaches and low backache are because you are dehydrated. Our bodies are made of approximately 70 per cent water so we need to replenish this daily. Most of us spend a fortune on expensive moisturisers to keep our face especially looking young – enough water daily will do wonders!

4. Cut down to three cups of tea or coffee a day. If you drink more than that, you cannot be getting enough water into your system. Tea, coffee and carbonated drinks are diuretics and so deplete the water in your system. Herbal teas, fruit and juices increase it.

5. Use honey instead of sugar in your tea or on your cereal. Unfortunately, there is very little nutritional merit in white processed sugar and the amount you take will affect your insulin levels. Good honey is a healthy alternative. Remember half a teaspoonful or less is all you need.

6. Steam, grill or stir-fry your food to maximise flavour and nutrients.

7. Try not to buy sweets, cakes or biscuits for home. You don't need them and neither do your children or teenagers (teach them about treats once a day or less).

8. Make sure you get out into the fresh air at least once a day for a walk. This is a great way to aerate the lungs and get the body moving.

BIBLIOGRAPHY

BOOKS

Kenny, R.A., *Age Proof: The New Science of Living a Longer and Healthier Life*, Lerum: Lagrom, 2022.

Kübler-Ross, E., *On Death and Dying*, London: Tavistock/Routledge, 1969.

McGoldrick, M. & Gerson, R., *Genograms: Assessment and Intervention*, London: W.W. Norton & Co., 1985.

Mee, P. & O'Brien, K., *Your Middle Years*, Dublin: Gill, 2016.

Northrup, C., *The Wisdom of Menopause*, New York: Bantam Dell, 2021.

Ornish, D., *Dr Dean Ornish's Program for Reversing Heart Disease*, New York: Century, 1990.

Shilling, J., *The Stranger in the Mirror: A Memoir of Middle Age*, London: Chatto & Windus, 2011.

WEBSITES

The Bealtaine Festival: www.bealtaine.ie

The Elisabeth Kübler-Ross Foundation: www.ekrfoundation.org

Irish Senior Citizens Parliament: www.seniors.ie

Dr Dean Ornish's Preventive Medicine Research Institute: www.pmri.org

Ornish Lifestyle Medicine: www.ornish.com

Senior Times (Ireland's website for people who don't act their age): www.seniortimes.ie

EVENTS

The Bealtaine Festival is a national celebration of creativity in older age and runs throughout the month of May annually (www.bealtaine.ie).

SeniorTimes Live! is a dedicated national consumer event for older people and runs in locations all over Ireland (www.seniortimes.ie/50-plus expo/).